Symbolic Misery

For Jean-Francois Peyret

Symbolic Misery

Volume 1
The Hyper-industrial Epoch

Bernard Stiegler

Translated by Barnaby Norman

polity

First published in French as *De la misère symbolique: Tome 1, L'époque hyperindustrielle* © Editions Galilée, 2004

This English edition © Polity Press, 2014

Polity Press
65 Bridge Street
Cambridge CB2 1UR, UK

Polity Press
350 Main Street
Malden, MA 02148, USA

ISBN-13: 978-0-7456-5264-1
ISBN-13: 978-0-7456-5265-8 (pb)

A catalogue record for this book is available from the British Library.

Typeset in 11 on 13 pt Sabon
by Toppan Best-set Premedia Limited
Printed and bound in Great Britain by Clays Ltd, St Ives PLC

The publisher has used its best endeavours to ensure that the URLs for external websites referred to in this book are correct and active at the time of going to press. However, the publisher has no responsibility for the websites and can make no guarantee that a site will remain live or that the content is or will remain appropriate.

Every effort has been made to trace all copyright holders, but if any have been inadvertently overlooked the publisher will be pleased to include any necessary credits in any subsequent reprint or edition.

For further information on Polity, visit our website: www.politybooks.com

Contents

There is a night in the night

Joë Bousquet

Such an adventure leaves some indifferent, because, they imagine, with a little greater or lesser rarity or sublimity in the pleasure people feel, that there is no change in the situation of what, alone, is most immeasurably precious and highest, known by the name of Poetry: it will always remain excluded, and the quiver of its wings elsewhere than on the page is parodied, not more, by the breadth, in our hands, of the hasty and vast pages of the newspaper. To gauge today's extraordinary overproduction, in which the Press cedes its means intelligently, the notion nevertheless prevails, that something very decisive is being elaborated . . .[1]

Stéphane Mallarmé

Foreword

This work continues my consideration, initiated in *Aimer, s'aimer, nous aimer. Du 11 septembre au 21 avril* [*Love, Love Yourself, Love One Another: From 11 September to 21 April*],[2] of the destruction of primordial narcissism brought about by the channelling of consumers' libido towards objects of consumption.

Our epoch is characterized by the seizure of the symbolic by industrial technology, where aesthetics has become both theatre and weapon in the economic war. This has resulted in a misery where conditioning substitutes for experience.

This misery is a disgrace, which has occasionally been experienced by the philosopher as 'one of the most powerful incentives towards philosophy, and what makes all philosophy political.'[3] The 'shame of being a man'[4] is provoked first of all, today, by this symbolic misery as engendered by 'control societies'. In this respect at least, this two-volume work is a commentary on the 'Postscript on Control Societies' by Gilles Deleuze, who, in order to understand the historic trends producing the specificity of the present, sought to sketch the concepts of *general organology* and *aesthetic genealogy*.

The first chapter, which introduces this idea, takes up and develops an article first published in *Le Monde* newspaper.

The second chapter develops the question of cinema and recorded song as industrial temporal objects through an analysis of *Same Old Song* [*On connaît la chanson*], a film by Alain Resnais.

The third chapter goes further into the question of the loss of individuation, attempting to outline a brief history of Western psychic and collective individuation by returning to the concept of *grammatization* put forward by Sylvain Auroux. The *process* of grammatization, distinctive of Western individuation and of the war over the control of symbols that constitute it, has passed through various epochs, the latest being commensurate with digitalization. This is the technological infrastructure of control societies, the stakes of which are analysed by way of an 'allegory of the anthill' that extrapolates the tendency inherent in networks towards hyper-synchronization and the *particularization of the singular* (as its negation), which is to say the decomposition of the diachronic and the synchronic. This chapter is the heart of the work.

The fourth chapter, inspired by *Tiresia*, a film by Bertrand Bonello, seeks to demonstrate that cinema occupies a unique position in the temporal war that is the cause of contemporary symbolic misery: at once industrial technology and art, cinema is the aesthetic experience that can combat aesthetic conditioning on its own territory.

An afterword looks at the situation of symbolic misery from a strictly political point of view, with reference to the three-part question of 21 April 2002 in France, conflict as the driving force of all political life, and *philia* today.

I

Of Symbolic Misery, the Control of Affects, and the Shame that Follows

It is not a case of worrying or hoping for the best, but of finding new weapons.

Gilles Deleuze

1. Aesthetics and politics

The question of politics is a question of aesthetics and, vice versa, the question of aesthetics is a question of politics. I use the word aesthetics here in its widest sense, where *aisthēsis* means sensory perception, and where the question of aesthetics is, therefore, that of feeling and sensibility in general.[1]

I maintain that we need to return to the question of aesthetics, particularly regarding its connection with the question of politics, in an appeal to the art-world to recover a political understanding of its role. The abandonment of the question of politics by the art-world is a catastrophe.

And likewise, the political world's abandonment of the question of aesthetics to the culture industry, and the market in general, is also catastrophic.[2]

Obviously I do not mean that artists should become politically 'engaged'. I mean that their work is *originally engaged* in the question of the *sensibility of the other*. The question of politics is essentially that of the relation to the other in a feeling-together or *sym-pathy*. The problem of politics is one of knowing how to be together, to live together, to stand each other and stand together, across and starting from our singularities (much more profound than our 'differences') and beyond our conflicts of interest. Politics is the art of securing the unity of the state in its *desire* for a common future, in its in-dividuation, its singularity as becoming-one. Such a desire assumes a common aesthetic ground: being together is feeling together. A political community is, therefore, a community of feeling. If we are unable to love things together (landscapes, towns, objects, works, languages, etc.), then we cannot love ourselves. This is the meaning of *philia* in Aristotle. Loving ourselves is loving together things other than ourselves.

The question of 'culture', as it is formulated in its essence by art, is now more than ever at the heart of the economy, of industry, and of politics: the *sensible* community is today entirely fabricated by the *technologies* of what Deleuze called 'control societies';[3] and it is essentially on this front that the international economic struggle is taking place.

Jacques Rancière has rightly noted that 'politicity' is sensible; that the question of politics is immediately aesthetic.[4] But he has strangely overlooked that the sensibility of the industrial era, bombarded as it is by marketing, has become the stake in a veritable war, in which the weapons are technologies and where the victims are individual and collective ('cultural') singularities. And that this has resulted in the development of a massive symbolic misery.

In today's control societies (also modulation societies),[5] aesthetic weapons play an essential role (this is what Jeremy Rifkin has referred to as 'cultural capitalism'): it has become a matter of controlling the technologies of *aisthēsis* (the audiovisual or the digital, for example) and, in this way, *controlling the conscious and unconscious rhythms of bodies and souls; modulating* through the control of flows these rhythms of consciousness and life. It is in this same context that the concept of *life time value* has recently been invented by marketing, as the *economically calculable* value of an individual lifetime (which amounts to the desingularization and disindividuation of its *intrinsic* value).

Breaking with tradition, Manet introduced a feeling which was not shared by everyone – and from the nineteenth century onwards aesthetic conflicts multiplied. But these conflicts, taking place against the backdrop of the massive industrial transformation of society, engendered a process of *sympathy construction*, which is characteristic of human aesthetics: a creativity transforms the world in view of building a new communal sensibility, forming the *inquiring 'us'* of an aesthetic community to come. We might call this an *aesthetic experience* as realized by art – in the same way as we speak of scientific investigation [*expérience*]: it aims at the *discovery of an-other feeling*, its *future bearing*.[6]

I believe, however, that aesthetic ambition in this sense has today largely collapsed. And this is because a huge proportion of the population is totally subjected to the aesthetic *conditioning* of marketing, now hegemonic for the vast majority of the world, and is, therefore, estranged from any *experience* of aesthetic investigation. Meanwhile, the other part of the population, that part that continues to experiment, has turned its back on those who founder in this conditioning.

It was on the day after 21 April 2002 that I was suddenly struck by this problem. On that day I saw with terrifying clarity that the people who voted for Jean-Marie Le Pen are people *with whom I feel nothing*, as though between us there is no common aesthetic experience. I realized that these men and women, these young people, *have no feeling* for what is happening, and for this reason they *no longer feel part of society*. They inhabit a *zone* (of whatever form of 'organization': commercial, industrial, even rural, etc.) which is no longer a *world* because aesthetically it has *disengaged*. 21 April was a politico-aesthetic catastrophe. These people, who are in a situation of severe symbolic misery, cannot stand the way modern society is going. In particular they loathe its aesthetic – *when it is not industrial*. And this is because *aesthetic conditioning*, the essential feature of enclosure in these zones, has replaced aesthetic experience, making it *impossible*.

It is important to realize that contemporary art, contemporary music, show business and the 'freelancers' of contemporary show business, along with contemporary literature, contemporary philosophy, and contemporary science, are a cause of suffering for the *ghetto* formed by these zones.

This misery is not limited to the poor: these zones are *everywhere*, spread like leprosy, in particular via television networks, giving concrete existence to Nietzsche's words: 'The desert grows'.

For all that, not everyone is exposed in the same way to the illness: while huge swathes of the population live in urban spaces stripped of all urbanity, a tiny minority enjoy an existence worthy of the name.

We should not think that the new destitute are terrible barbarians. They are the very heart of consumer society. They are *civilization*. But only inasmuch as, paradoxically, its *heart* has become a ghetto. Now this ghetto is humiliated, insulted by what has happened. And we, supposedly cultured people, scholars, artists, philosophers, perceptive and well informed as we are, we have to understand that the vast majority of society lives in this state of symbolic misery, marked by humiliation and insult. This is the havoc wrought by the *aesthetic war* that follows the hegemonic rule of the market. The vast majority of society lives in aesthetically afflicted zones where aesthetic alienation makes it *impossible* to live and love oneself.

I know this world well: it is where I come from. And I know that it bears within it unimaginable energy. But left abandoned this energy will become destructive.

In the twentieth century a new aesthetics was established which *functionalized the affective and aesthetic dimension of the individual* so as to produce a *consumer*. This process had other aspects too: some aimed at making a believer, others a devotee to power, and still others a free thinker, exploring the boundlessness that echoes in the body at the sensible encounter of world and becoming.

It certainly is not a matter of condemning the industrial and technological fate of humanity. Rather, it is a case of reinventing this fate. To this end it is necessary to gain an understanding of the situation in which aesthetic conditioning developed, which, if it is not overcome, will generate a general revulsion and the collapse of consumption itself.

It is possible to distinguish at least two kinds of aesthetics: there is that of the psycho-physiologists who study the sense organs; and that of the history of art, of artefacts, symbols and works. While the psycho-physiological aesthetic appears stable, that of the artefact evolves continually through time. But the stability of the sense organs is an illusion inasmuch as they are subjected to a never-ending process of defunctionalization and refunctionalization which is tied, precisely, to the evolution of artefacts.

The aesthetic history of humanity amounts to a series of successive dis-adjustments between the three great organizational structures that together constitute man's aesthetic power: the body with its physiological organization; artificial organs (technologies, objects, tools, instruments, artworks); and social organizations resulting from the articulation of artefacts and bodies.

It is necessary to conceive a general organology which would study the joint history of these three dimensions of human aesthetics, along with the resulting tensions, inventions and potentials. These would be the initial considerations of a project such as I am attempting to outline here.

Only this kind of genealogical approach allows us to understand the aesthetic evolution leading to today's symbolic misery – where we affirm in hope that a new force lies concealed, as much in the *extraordinary opening of possibility* brought by science and technology as in the *affect of suffering itself*.

So what happened to the affective domain in the twentieth century? In order to absorb the over-production of unnecessary goods, the 1940s saw American industry implementing marketing techniques first envisaged by Freud's nephew Edward Bernays in the 1930s. These techniques became increasingly advanced throughout the rest of the century as returns on investments were made on economies of scale requiring ever bigger mass markets.

In order to reach these markets, industry developed an aesthetic particularly well adapted to audiovisual media, which *refunctionalized* the aesthetic dimension of the individual according to the interests of industrial development, causing him to adopt the behaviours of consumerism.

The resulting symbolic misery is also a libidinal and affective misery, which leads to the *loss* of what I call *primordial narcissism*,[7] whereby individuals are stripped of their ability to form aesthetic attachments to singularities or singular objects.

Locke foresaw in the seventeenth century that I am singular through the singularity of the objects with which I am in relation. I *am* the *relationship* with my objects inasmuch as it is *singular*. But the relationship with the standardized objects of industry is 'profiled' and categorized into *particularisms* which, for the purposes of marketing, constitute market segments. In this way *the singular is transformed into the particular*, laying the ground for communitarianisms of all kinds. For *the particularization of the singular is its annulment* and strictly speaking its *liquidation* in the *flow* of commodity-fetish.[8]

The audiovisual techniques of marketing lead, moreover, to a situation where, through the images I see and the sounds I hear, my past tends to become the same as my neighbour's. And the diversification of channels is simply the particularization of targets – which explains why they all tend to do the same thing. Being increasingly constituted by the images and sounds that the media streams through my consciousness, as well as by the objects (and relationships with these objects) that these images lead me to consume, my past is less and less differentiated from that of other people. It loses, therefore, its singularity, which is as much as to say, I lose myself as singularity.

Once I am deprived of my singularity I can no longer love myself: it is only possible to love oneself starting from the intimate knowledge of one's own singularity. And this is why 'the community originally consists in the intimacy of the bond between self and self.'[9] Art is the *experience* and the *support* of this sensible singularity as an invitation to symbolic activity, to the production and discovery of traces in collective time.

And this is why the question of aesthetics, the question of politics, and the question of industry together form one question.

2. The symbolic in the age of consumerism: A global misery

Hominization, as the pursuit of life by means other than life, is the appearance of a form of communal existence where the *distribution of roles* is based not only on genetics but on individual *fates* [*destins*] (of *existences* and their *ancestries*, which is to say the past as it acts in them), establishing themselves in a history which is no longer that of a simple species. Hominization is the *functional externalization of individual and singular experiences* which are then transmitted to descendants, who are thus established as inheritors.

I am speaking here as much about the hand gestures of flint cutters as of those of the later cave painters: it is this singularity of existences (*ex-sistere* is maintaining oneself outside of oneself) that is conserved and transmitted by technical objects like paintings and cut tools. And, however differently, this therefore makes them first and foremost memory supports, if not mnemotechnics properly speaking (I will return to this theme, which was also Nietzsche's).

Now, it seems very likely that since the dawn of hominization, the collective individuation constitutive of a society has presupposed the *participation* of the all in the production of the *one*, or the whole. This is the fantasy and the fiction necessary for establishing the theatre of supposed unity we call 'society'. And this is done by way of a social *dimension* such as language, religion, family structure, mode of production, etc. We might call these structures, systems or apparatuses, but they always presuppose an *originary exteriorization* which is the support of individual fates [*destins*].

These *means* by which the *one* is constituted as the fantasy of a whole, these *dimensions*, signify that society, as such, does not exist, nor community. It is nothing but the arrangement of apparatuses or systems. In order to produce the *one*, however, this arrangement must itself be the bearer of a singularity which is idiomatic, or in other words both singular and communal.

These arrangements are supported by what I have called *epiphylogenetic* strata or tertiary retentions. That is to say, the *concretions* of knowledge and abilities in objects and devices passed on as *things belonging to the human world*. In this way they include a mnemo-technical dimension, even if they are not properly speaking mnemotechnics. A builder's shovel or a pitchfork as I might use them day-to-day have no mnemonic function, but they nevertheless bear the memory of gestures and functions, and through this they are automatically projected into the mnemo-technical stratum of all things inasmuch as they belong to a world.

Mnemotechnics properly speaking appear after the Neolithic age and immediately become the organizational tool of power. But, with the constitution of the Greek city state, and later the Christian church, these tools, which I have previously called *retentional*, are in the hands of administrators (legal and religious, political and spiritual) who determine the criteria of selection (canon law, correct formulations, correct gestures, correct actions, good morals and procedures, etc.). They are thought of in terms of a process of individuation presupposing the *participation* of the many in the *production* of the one, albeit under the authority of administrators.

It is in the nineteenth century that mnemo*technologies* make their first appearance. Technologies and no longer simply technics, these are the industrial products and machines which open the audiovisual era (the photograph and the phonograph, cinema, radio and television). Then, in the twentieth century (following from Hollerith's work on data-processing) come the technologies of calculation, and the mnemo-techno-logical becomes the *actual support of industrial life*, fully subjected to the imperatives of the global, mechanical, division of labour – *a fortiori* since by way of generalized digitalization the technologies of information and communication converge to form the context for what we today call 'cultural' or 'cognitive' capitalism.

Now, among the social roles newly distributed by the industrial revolution a previously unheard-of requirement emerged: the need to *offload* the products of industry coming in ever increasing numbers from thermodynamic, then electric and electronic, mechanization. These products are increasingly diverse yet also, and simultaneously, ever more standardized, *thus changing the nature of diversity*.

This job of offloading is entrusted to marketing which, from the nineteenth century (even if it is not really defined as such until the twentieth century), seizes on mnemotechnologies to assure the proper *functioning* of the system. That is, the always *accelerating* (and more entropic: and herein lies the problem) *circulation* of the energies on which it is founded.

But these energies are here no longer involved in the symbolic *circulation* of participation, establishing the sym-bol (*sum-bolon* in Greek) as sensible, cognitive and spiritual sharing (spiritual in the sense of spirits which *come back*, deferring and enduring in repetition). The *functional circulation of energies* in control societies (which, by *controlling bodies and their affects* produce consumers, this being the goal of the system as it offloads products and organizes the adoption of incessant novelties – the innovations of what we call modernity) engenders the *loss of symbolic participation*. This is also a kind of *symbolic and affective congestion*.

That is, and I come back to this in Chapter III, 'Allegory of the Anthill', the structural loss of individuation that I began to analyse in *Love, Love Yourself, Love One Another: From 11th September to 21st April.* It is the circuit of desire that is thus destroyed. In other words, *desire itself* is destroyed because it can no longer be a circuit: the circuit of a gift (I will return to this in *Symbolic Misery 2*).[10] From here comes the general feeling of disarray prevalent everywhere, where hatred of self and others grows and people carry out the kind of murderous act shown so well by Gus Van Sant's film *Elephant* (2003) – here are the fruits of the death drive, along with their strange pleasure.

With the appearance of marketing, taking place at about the same time as Fordism, it is no longer only a matter of the reproduction of the producer (of his labour force, energy sources, primary materials, etc. – everything that Marx thought about), but also the fabrication, reproduction, diversification and segmentation of consumer needs.

The existential energies (existences of producers and consumers) which assure the functioning of the system are the products of the desire – the *libido* – of producers on one side and consumers on the other. Work, like consumption, *is libido captured and channelled.* Work in general is sublimation and the reality principle – and this includes, of course, artistic work. But proletarian work and industrial labour more generally have nothing to do with art, or even craft: quite the contrary. And the consumer whose libido is captured derives less and less pleasure from consuming: he *softens* [*débande*], numbed by the compulsion to repeat, of which bulimia and anorexia present strange cases (as did, at the time of Hitler, in the paradoxical and archaic age of industry, the eels in *The Tin Drum* by Günter Grass). It is not by chance that it is right now that obesity has become the subject of debate, being as it is the devastating result of the exploitation of bodies, along with their passions, frustrations and drives.[11]

This is happening because the industrialization of audiovisual and informational mnemotechnologies, which made the aesthetico-industrial war possible, while constituting marketing's arsenal, has led inevitably to the *industrial* division of labour – also affecting roles outside the workplace such as the relationship with 'products', here with symbols (cognitive or aesthetic) – and this has led to an opposition between the 'producers' and the 'consumers' of these symbols; an opposition which kills desire.

This is why cultural capitalism (both informational and cognitive) is the most worrying problem imaginable for industrial ecology:[12] the mental, intellectual, affective and aesthetic capacities of humanity are massively threatened, and this at just the same time that human groups have an unprecedented power of destruction at their disposal. The ecological crisis resulting from the industrial production of symbols opens the epoch of global symbolic misery, and this affects (although in very different ways) the North as much as the South and what we must now *distinguish* as the Extreme-Orient.

By symbolic misery I mean, therefore, the loss of individuation which results from the *loss of participation* in the *production of symbols*.[13] Symbols here being as much the fruits of intellectual life (concepts, ideas, theorems, knowledge) as of sensible life (arts, know-how, mores). And I believe that the present state of generalized loss of individuation can only lead to a symbolic collapse, or the collapse of desire – in other words to the decomposition of the social as such: to total war.

3.　The control of affects and war

It is a matter of 'finding new weapons' writes Deleuze as he formulates the concept of *control societies* in 1990. By way of this concept he describes what comes to pass[14] with what I will call (in Chapter III) the *hyper-industrial* age (and not, we will see why, the 'postmodern' age).

The question *of weapons* is the question *of technics in general.* When the question of technics is posed *as a question*, and as a question concerning the fate of a *we*, when it is posed, in other words, as a question of *techne* (which is also that of making and knowhow, of art and artwork, and therefore of the sensible *as fiction*), this *question* of technics opens the question of *politics* as the attempt to pacify a conflict which, in life generally, is a 'struggle for life' and which, in the history of technical life itself, of 'human' life, is a war that mortals make with themselves.[15]

Indeed, it is because they are threatened by the fate bestowed by their originary 'prostheticity' (the fate of their neoteny we would say today), which leads them to make war among themselves, that, via Hermes, Zeus sends knowledge of law to the mortal technicians. That this message should be carried by the god of the secret, of the enigma and of hermeneutics (to which he gives his name) signifies that this knowledge is at the same time that of a non-knowledge and that of an always open and continuous interpretation of this non-knowledge, which *makes* the law. This is what I sought to establish in *The Fault of Epimetheus*.[16]

It is, therefore, subject to interpretation or discernment, that is to say *krinein* ('judgement'), that war, inherent in technics to the extent that it is always weaponry, can transform itself into *peaceful political struggle* in this sense. In the space, that is, of rights – which is also the space of a *we*.

In *Disorientation*[17] I examined in more detail how the condition of constitution of such a *we*, inasmuch as it *questions* the *we*, which is to say inasmuch as it is politically open, is to be found in a particular kind of technics, in an arsenal that deserves a particular approach: the mnemotechnics[18] that enable the law to be written, its literal establishment, open the public space of the we, the we as *res publica*. Hermes is the god of this arsenal that I then referred to as the literal synthesis of the memory of the *we*, which is a kind of retentional apparatus (in the sense expounded in *Cinematic Time and the Question of Malaise*).[19]

War takes place with the failure of political pacification – which always remains, whatever the case may be, the *agora* of a struggle, of an agonistic or an eristic, the art of dispute. In times of peace as of war, *polemos*, of which *eris* is the civil and regulated version, is the law of all things: the law of becoming.

Today we are at war and – we all feel this – are close to falling away from politics. We have already *descended* to a new kind of war, where all of us have reason to feel the shame of being a man. This war without like, with the affect at its heart, is protean and unprecedented in its forms. A war may be civil, interethnic, interreligious or international, it is never political: politics is not war, but precisely its avoidance through the legal affirmation of a *we* which is always in itself polemical. But, says Aristotle, such an affirmation cannot only be legal. It implies *philia*, which is a feeling of the *we*, the feeling it has of *making-us*. To which I would add that it implies two other feelings: a feeling for that which is unjust – *dikē* is first of all encountered as a lack of justice, where justice defaults[20] – and a feeling of humility, of honour or of shame [*honte*] as we say with regard to *aidós*, which I prefer, however, to translate as *reserve* [*vergogne*].[21]

Such *feelings* are supported by aesthetics as *sym-pathy*, the condition of all *philia*.

But – and *this is the organological crux of aesthetics and politics alike* – reserve [*vergogne*] and the feeling of injustice (of the 'iniquity' of things, *tēs adikias*, the only 'word' of Anaximander's that we know), where the feeling of justice is established *by default*, suggest that *philia* is the experience of the *we* as prostheticity, the originary *default* of the origin, which is to say the *default of a tie that would be inalienable and infallible*. That which here binds the political *we* is always already the knowledge of its *fragility* – the *non-knowledge* that is the condition of shame, or of what I call reserve [*vergogne*]. And this fragility is the lot of those who are born to prostheticity, to technics as the destiny granted them by the fault of Epimetheus, compounded by that of Prometheus when he stole the fire. Man is a thief by proxy, by prosthetic destiny.

This prosthetic destiny does not arise in the twentieth century, as we might think from a cursory reading of *Civilisation and its Discontents*, but represents the originary default of the origin that is the *originary murder* of the father by the weapon that is all technics. And the first of these technics is the knife, that of *Totem and Taboo* just as much as that of the sacrifice of Isaac, but which Freud, not knowing how, was unable to think.

Reserve [*vergogne*], however, or shame [*honte*], the very thing that imposes hospitality, the welcoming of suppliants, but which also, as a malaise [*malaise*] in culture (*Kulture*), or as what I have called ill-being [*mal-être*],[22] offends the narcissistic pride of the human *we*,[23] is never simply that of the *we* turned in on itself. It is rather that of a *we* that is capable of exiling itself without fleeing, of exceeding itself in the *distance* or in the *excess* of an outside, as a tearing away (as the 'vertigo of tearing away'), which is also the opening to what has been called the universal, *to catholou*.

But, deterritorialized (this is the *doing* of the tearing away), this *we* is today closed on itself as the *maddening vanity of a globe – such is the distortion of the question of the universality* of the *we* that undoes itself *for want of philia.*[24] What is there of reserve [*vergogne*] (and the narcissism it presupposes) in control societies?

> And we can feel shame at being human in utterly trivial situations, too: in the face of too great a vulgarisation of thinking, in the face of TV entertainment, of a ministerial speech, of "jolly people" gossiping. This is one of the most powerful incentives towards philosophy, and it's what makes all philosophy political. In capitalism only one thing is universal, the market. There's no universal state, precisely because there's a universal market of which states are the centres, the trading floors. But the market's not universalising, homogenising, it's an extraordinary generator of both wealth and misery. A concern for human rights shouldn't lead us to extol the "joys" of the liberal capitalism of which they're an integral part. There's no democratic state that's not compromised to the very core by its part in generating human misery. What's so shameful is that we've no way of *maintaining becomings, or still more of arousing them, even within ourselves.*[25]

Because the war that today has made us abandon all reserve [*vergogne*] is economic. And this economy is an alienation of desire and of affects, where the weaponry is organized by marketing:

> Marketing is now the instrument of social control.[26]

As the space of an international struggle, the economy has become a war without rules, where civilians and combatants are indistinguishable, where the *contract* that can always be broken substitutes for the *law*, where piracy is widespread and where arsenals have evolved such that the war has become *essentially aesthetic* – which not only does not prevent military, religious, interethnic or international conflicts, but clearly incubates and heralds them.

This aesthetic war, which is also, and to begin with, a temporal war, is at the heart of what Deleuze called control societies – conceived here initially in terms of the *control of affects* (that is to say of time, of auto-affection).

II

As Though We Were Lacking[1]
or How to Find Weapons in Alain Resnais' *Same Old Song*

4. Ill-being and respect

I would like to show you a film, or my vision of a film which, I
believe, stages like no other the ill-being of our epoch. I am talking
about *Same Old Song*, a work by Alain Resnais. I believe, and I
would like to demonstrate to you, that the ill-being it stages bears
an essential relationship with the cultural industries, with cinema,
with television and with music. Before tackling these issues, I
would like to refer to an article that I read in the newspaper
Libération this morning (2 May 2002) when I was coming here
on the train from Paris to Lyon. This article, you have probably
guessed, is about the current situation in French politics. Like
many others at the moment, it attempts to analyse the motivations
of the people who voted for the National Front on 21 April last
year in France. In this instance, the inhabitants of the village of
Bessan in the Hérault. It is the protocol of this exhibition, of its
organizational mode, that the press should be present, as you see
and experience yourselves from the sheets of newspaper on which
you are sitting and lying. I read one of these sheets this morning
and I would like to make a few remarks.

A journalist from *Libération* is questioning an inhabitant of
Bessan, Bernard, who is employed part time on a short-term contract in a school canteen. The journalist asks him to introduce
himself and to explain why he voted for the National Front. In
his reply, Bernard

first of all points out that he is neither 'someone from the right nor the extreme right', and that he is 'more to the left, even, and a pacifist', but that he has had enough of this society. '*It couldn't be worse than it is at the moment*, there is no security here, including employment. I'm in favour of Europe, but Europe does nothing for fishing and winemaking. In Pézenas the police take pot shots at each other, in Bessan the mayor was attacked, in Paris they [*we* don't know who he is talking about exactly – and yet *we* know] whistle the *Marseillaise*, here the kids climb on the statue of Marianne, there is no respect anymore, none at all.'

'There is no respect anymore, none at all.' I am going to try to speak to you about *this*. In other words, what I am going to speak about is at the heart of the current political situation in France. I believe that the question posed to *each one of us today, whether or not we voted for the National Front*, is one of an immense disorientation, an immense confusion, a *great ill-being* – an ill-being that is staged by the film I am about to present.

5. Aesthetics and insecurity

I would like to highlight and analyse this ill-being beyond any particular, effective, cause. It is undeniable that there are a thousand different causes that might lead people to vote for the National Front, among which what we call insecurity, for example, is not simply imaginary. There are, of course, problems with insecurity in France and in the wider world: there are problems with insecurity in Iraq, for example, there are problems in Afghanistan, and in Palestine and Israel. There are also problems with insecurity in Paris, in Lyon and in Bessan.

But these problems, particularly here in France, only lead people to vote for the National Front because the *aesthetic apparatus of socialization and the feeling of a* we *which it alone can engender are now extremely fragile, if not completely destroyed*. It is because of the *aesthetic apparatus of socialization* that men and women live together, *are able to* live together, or, in other words, are able to feel together, to share in sensitivity, and say 'we'. And this *we* can sometimes designate humanity in its totality, even if, as a rule, this *we* only designates *a part* of the whole, while at the same time, however, aiming always beyond this part, proclaiming in some way the whole, be it in the name of God.

This 'apparatus' and this 'feeling' started moving towards destruction the moment *the aesthetic became the object of a systematic industrial exploitation*, with the exclusive and hegemonic aim, in Gramsci's sense, of *developing the markets of consumption*. This has resulted in the transformation of the sentient body, the sensitive body, the desiring body, into *a consuming body whose desire, I hazard, is led to ruin* – through its absolutely systematic exploitation by the culture industries, marketing, and everything that an unfortunate candidate in the French presidential elections (who certainly didn't undertake the analyses I am suggesting here) thought to call the 'market society'.

This systematic exploitation of sensitivity leads to the ruin of body and soul, of which the vote for the National Front is only a symptom – among many others, less evident and seemingly less terrifying. In other words, we encounter here the enormous problems brought about by what I have referred to as the industrial ecology of the spirit.[2]

The nineteenth century saw the birth of large-scale industry which systematically exploited natural resources to develop an industry of material goods for consumption. The twentieth century was the century of Hollywood, of large-scale mass-media, of artificial intelligence, of information industries – or the *development of an industry which made consciousness and spirit its 'raw materials'*. A consumer is first of all a consciousness and this consciousness is 'spiritual', in the sense that it is constituted by *a spirit* (a culture, an epoch) and by *spirits* (predecessors, ancestors, traces). In order to sell the cars of Ford or Chrysler, the soda of Coca-Cola or Schweppes, the information machines of Apple or IBM, the services of France Télécom or America On Line, ready-to-wear clothes, shoes, toothpaste or trips to Turkey, to Corsica or to Poitou-Charentes, it is necessary to speak to consciousnesses: these consciousnesses are markets, they are the *driving force* of these markets – and this inasmuch as they are bodies and bodies that have desires.

Today, consciousnesses have essentially become 'raw material', allowing access to the markets of consumption. Inasmuch as they determine access to the behaviour of consuming bodies, consciousnesses (and the spirit in which they are immersed) constitute *a meta-market, the market which gives access to all other markets*, whatever they may be, and including, therefore, financial markets. Consciousnesses and spirits have become the objects of a systematic, world-wide, exploitation, led by global groups that have taken hold of industries such as cinema, radio and television – and, in so doing, industrial *song*, which is to say *recorded* song that is produced and broadcast by the culture industries.

This, then, is what I want to talk to you about, at the invitation of my friend Sarkis.

6.   Recap on industrial temporal objects

We are living in the epoch of what I call industrial temporal objects. I have already expounded the concept elsewhere, but I think it is worth going over it again, both for the benefit of the listener or reader, and so as to consider a variation on an established theme – the variation here being *song*.

A temporal object is constituted by the time of its flow – as, for example, is the case with a musical melody, a cinematic film, a radio broadcast, etc. An object is temporal, in the Husserlian sense, to the extent that it is *constituted* by the flow of its passing, as opposed to an object like a piece of chalk, which is constituted through its stability, by the fact that it does not flow.

A temporal object like a melody only appears in its disappearance: it is an object that passes, and that in this sense bears a remarkable relationship to its passing, and also, therefore, to a question of the past. In the same way, a film only appears *to the extent that* it disappears, and according to the *manner* of its disappearance: the disappearance is not uniform. Depending on the temporal object and the person who creates it, it marks different styles.

The temporal object is very interesting for anyone who studies consciousness, to the extent that it too is temporal in this sense. The temporal object, a film for example, has the same structure as you inasmuch as you are in the process of listening to me,[3] and this, *to the extent that* you are *consciousnesses*. You yourselves, at this very moment, *you are in flux*, that is to say *disappearing so as to appear* – each person differently and each in a singular relationship to their particular past, and their particular passing, and also, therefore, to their future.

You had a beginning, and we call that your birth. You will have an end: this will be your death. Between your birth and your death, *while awaiting your individual death*, and *following your individual birth*, you are in flux, you pass – which is also what we call *learning*. You arrived here between three o'clock and three fifteen, and you are going to spend a little time with me – half an hour, an hour, three hours – and then, this will be over, and you will move on to something else. And what happened will never happen again, it *will be forever past, you will never be able to return*.

I am fifty years old, and I can never be twenty again. Neither can you. *WE are, together, temporal: it is what binds us*. It is, without doubt, the only thing. But it is a *very powerful* bond. And very *sensitive*. And yet, I am going to show you, *this bond is seriously threatened*.

The microphone that I have in my hand is also deteriorating. If you were to find this microphone in a hundred years it would probably be rusted and broken. It is subject to the law of what physicists call entropy: it is destined to dispersal and one day or another it will turn to dust. But this microphone remains stable in its appearance: if I am able to use it at this moment, it is precisely because it is stable. If, between the time I start and the time I finish using it, it were to change structure, then that would be very problematic, and we would say that this microphone does not work, because, in fact, it would be unusable. This is something that we experience with the liquefaction of clocks in some of Dali's paintings.

A temporal object, as opposed to this microphone (and these clocks, but they raise particular issues), is constituted by the fact that, *like our consciousnesses*, it flows and disappears as it appears.

7. At the cinema

Today, at the beginning of the twenty-first century, a huge proportion of industrial activity is engaged in the production of temporal objects, characterized by the fact that they appear in their disappearance, which is to say that they *coincide in the time of their flow with the time of your consciousness.* When you watch a film or a television show, when you listen to a radio broadcast or a song, the time of the flow of the temporal object you are considering, that your consciousness is taking as its object, this time flows with the flow of the time of your consciousness which is interlaced with it.

This coincidence of the temporal flow of your consciousness with the flow of temporal objects is what enables *your consciousness to ADOPT the time of the temporal objects in question.*

Imagine that you are at the cinema watching a thriller. You arrive at the beginning of the film and you have a toothache; you *feel* on arrival that you have a pain in this tooth – and then, as you enter into the film, you *forget* your tooth. Or again, if you are in a cinema with bad seats, and in the seat in which you are sitting a spring is causing you pain in your backside, as the film develops, as you enter into the film, *taking up and adopting the time of its flow,* you cease to think of your backside or your tooth. You *are no longer* in the seat, and your tooth is no longer in your mouth, or, rather, you are no longer in your body: you are *in the screen.* You are in the screen because you have adopted the time of the film.

It is this structure of temporal objects which also allows contemporary cultural industries to make you adopt the time of consumption of toothpaste, soda, shoes and cars, etc. This is how today's culture industry is almost exclusively financed. And this global industry of images poses the problems of industrial ecology, of consciousness and of spirit that I alluded to above. It ends up producing very critical, very serious, situations, and leads finally to the ruin of the *primordial narcissism* presupposed by all *philia.*

A consciousness is essentially a consciousness *of self,* that is, one that is able to say *I* – *I* am not the same as anyone else, I am a singularity, which means that *I give myself my own time.* If you are listening to me at the moment, it is because you are expecting something from me, something that you don't have: you expect something from my consciousness inasmuch as *it is not synchronized* with yours. But the cultural industries, and particularly television, constitute a massive synchronization machine. When people watch the same event on television, at the same time, live, in their tens of millions, even hundreds of millions, consciousnesses all over the world interiorize, adopt and live the same temporal objects at the same moment. When these consciousnesses repeat the same behaviours of audiovisual consumption every day, watching the same television shows, at the same time, with perfect regularity (because everything is so arranged), these 'consciousnesses' end up becoming that of the same person – that is, *nobody*. Nobody in the sense that Ulysses encounters the Cyclops. A Cyclops has only one eye: he has no perspective, no stereoscopic vision and for him everything is flattened: he has *neither depth of field, nor depth of time*. This Cyclops who sees *Nobody* is the figure of our ill-being.[4]

8. Song

Towards the end of 1996, the composer François Bayle suggested that I give a paper to the Musical Research Group at the National Audiovisual Institute [*l'Institute national de l'audiovisuel*] where he was then a director (I was myself a director of the NAI at that time). *Disorientation* had just come out, and not wanting simply to restate what I had already written on the subject of temporal objects, I decided to begin my talk with this provocative phrase:

The most important musical event of the twentieth century was recorded song.

This was not only a rhetorical gesture which, through the surprise I believed it would elicit in my audience, would allow me to keep their interest. I set out firmly and I still maintain that, at least in certain respects, the major musical occurrence of the twentieth century was that *masses of ears* suddenly started to listen to music – endlessly. Often the same standardized tunes, the overwhelming majority of which were 'easy-listening' – produced and reproduced in enormous quantities, they are what we now refer to as 'hits'. They make considerable fortunes and even lead to ennoblements. Often for several hours a day they intertwine with consciousnesses across the world, producing a *daily total of several billion hours of 'musicalized' consciousnesses* – whereas in previous centuries, access to musical temporal objects was generally rare, even exceptional, taking place in religious or celebratory contexts such as vespers or exclusive nocturnes.[5]

The musical twentieth century is singular, strange even, in many other respects. But, persuaded that music begins with the ear, with listening, I believe that, first and foremost, it is so from this perspective.[6] Because, while the first works of New Music were being composed, a *new listening*, emerging at the beginning of the twentieth century, and *made possible by the analogue recording of temporal musical objects, also profoundly altered the century's way of hearing*, including, first of all, that of musicians themselves – a literally *unheard-of* innovation which is never sufficiently accounted for (we, who have *always known reproducible* temporal objects, will *never be able* to account for it – no more than we would *ever* be able to *see* for the first time like a blind person recovering their sight; because even a blind person who recovers their sight, or a deaf person who recovers their hearing, *suffers* before they are able to hear or see, much more, and much sooner than they realize that they are suffering).

It is analogue recording *which enables both recorded song and cinema*, the two primary objects produced by the cultural industries[7] – which meet and intertwine in *Same Old Song*, and with which, in its turn, the consciousness of the spectator/listener is intertwined.

This film by Alain Resnais, which came out shortly after the 1996 conference, made an extraordinary impression on me. It revived and fortified both my recent interrogation of *recorded* song along with the kind of listening it produces, and my explorations in the field of cinema into Fellini's film *Interview* [*Intervista*].[8]

Recorded song and film are simultaneously temporal objects and mass products. They are produced by the cultural industries, and, like consciousness, are fluid. *Via the extension of radio and television* and because of *the scale of their industrial temporality*, they come to modify the temporality of that consciousness – that is to say, the totality of consciousness, which is *nothing but* temporality, being *process* through and through, and not a *stable* structure (this process, in its fluidity, nevertheless includes *meta-stabilized forms*, which become meta-structural, like whirlpools in the current which forms the basis of all this).

It is this *transformation of time, with time*, which Alain Resnais so admirably stages – and *as ill-being*.

In *Same Old Song*, one temporal object, recorded song, is presented in and by another temporal object, cinema, both of which are dependent on mechanical and analogue recording and reproducibility. The film seizes on, while significantly multiplying, transforming and, in a certain sense, *sublimating*, the particular effects produced by recorded song, which forms its subject. And it is the subject of extremely refined editing and sound mixing processes, which, through a game of re-contextualization and a very particular 'Kuleshov effect',[9] create a film which is both clear and complex, charming and unforgettable – the scene of a perfectly dramatic tension between laughter and tears.

9. We

We all know the songs being played here – 'we', that is, the audience *living in France*: all these songs are in French and sung by French people except for one, *What?*, performed by Jane Birkin. But this is a unique occurrence, enjoying in another respect a status of exception, to which I will return.

We all know the songs being played here and, in this sense, *we* are *present in the film*, and not only in the audience, in front of the screen. Not only are we present as *countless ears* that ring and resonate with each refrain from the mouths of the characters, in an echo that leaves us dumbfounded. But *it is the question of the* we *as such that this film explores like no other before it*, and with such overwhelming force. A question of the *we* which, *along with that of the adoption that this* we *implies*, forms the horizon of the thought I developed in *Cinematic Time and the Question of Malaise [mal-être]*.[10] Because the *idiomatic* mark of the song, an essential aspect of the dramatic concerns of the film, clearly opens an enormous question, explored in *Cinematic Time* as *this question of adoption*, which is to say of 'facticity' as well. This is what is carefully staged in the film in terms of what Resnais calls 'appearances'.

It is hard to imagine that someone watching this film who had never lived in France, and knew nothing, therefore, of its *popular culture*, would be able to see it – which necessarily involves both grasping it [*l'entendre*], and, as we will see, grasping it with the eyes. It would obviously be very easy, on the other hand, to imagine the film including foreign songs – if there is something striking about the role of song in the twentieth century it is surely the international circulation of idioms it produces. But this would have made for an entirely different film, exploring a broader notion of the *we*. And doubtless this would have been at the price of a less insistent focus on *its highest point of concentration*, which is always in relationship with a particular *place*.

Here, the place is Paris.

Most of the songs in the film are known to everyone (many of them are 'hits'). Throughout the eighty years since the first *terrestrial broadcasts* they have aired on French radios, and have been distributed commercially as *phonographic recordings*. They are *played* by the characters in the film. It could not be said that they are *sung* by them: they are only mimed. The singers are the people who created the songs: *Avec le temps*, for example, is sung here by Léo Ferré. These voices are appropriated such that they *ventriloquize* the characters at the same time as they *spectralize* the time of the film: they trigger an avalanche of *ghostly returns* [*une avalanche de revenances*].

Because it is not only the characters that are ventriloquized and haunted, but it is *in us* that the ghosts come back. These are the frequentations of a past that is sometimes very vague – floating memories, welling up in the tunes, refrains, melodies, interludes and words, which at times seem to us very beautiful, true and ultimately necessary, like authentic works of art. To us, that is, who bestow such little importance on these *organs* – the voices of the singers and the ear lent to them by our epoch; *our ear*.

10.   The air of an epoch – and the family

To the extent that they inhabit us as well, *we* ourselves are ventriloquized by these songs, and this *precisely to the extent that we form a we*. A *we* whose unity is simple and fairly weak, or 'impoverished' [*démuni*] as is said of an unpleasant character in the film (Marc Duverrier, played by Lambert Wilson). But which is richer than we might initially think, complex in its simplicity: this is what we discover as the film, with its songs, develops. And in this development the songs impose themselves as the colour, the tone, the fabric and in a way as the *air* of an epoch. But a 'funny kind of epoch'. This fluid and intangible realization is brought home to us over the course of the story, ultimately bringing us to a final act where songs follow on from each other in a rhythm dominated and then brought to an end by Claude François.

We share with the characters, therefore, something very indeterminate of their past: as they sing, they call up something of our own memories along with *their fabrication*, and we find ourselves included in their personalities and histories, as though we belonged to the same *family*.[11] I have already analysed a similar structure staged by Fellini in *Interview*. We will see how and why in Resnais' film the stratagem is *rigorously* bound to the fact that song, like film, is a *temporal* object, and an *industrial* temporal object – or in other words, a particular kind of 'tertiary retention'.[12]

Leaving the cinema having just watched and listened to *Same Old Song* – or turning off the television, video recorder, computer or DVD player – you get the irresistible urge to start singing. This desire only becomes apparent *after* the film. As it is happening, in the intimacy of our viewing consciousness, which listens *with its eyes*, we are too enthralled by the extraordinary necessity of the storyline and its dramatization, in which we are already so *implicated*, to be tempted to burst into song. Neither in the dark of the cinema, nor sheltered by our screens.

We are dealing with a serious film.

An immense drama is being played out here: ours.

11.   Clichés

By this device we are bound to the characters in a way that has not been possible in any previous film. It is an extraordinarily bold device, clear and indisputable in its effects, to the point of being charming in the midst of a great melancholy that is expressed in myriad ways and which touches us deeply. It is a drama filled with melodies, and therefore a *melodrama*, and yet it is above all a *tragicomedy*.

The characters are caught somewhere *between lip-synching* (miming the words to your own song which has been pre-recorded – a ploy typical of the variety shows through which song invaded television in the 1960s) and karaoke (taking the place of a singer, imitating them by singing along with their background music – a mass phenomenon which is also typical of an epoch and a certain symbolic misery). They are not *lip-synching* because, apart from Jane Birkin, they are not the songs' singers: they do not pretend to be them. Neither, like a karaoke singer, do they pretend to be them for the 'duration of a song'. What they are doing is both much more complex and much more banal; they are, LIKE US (although *we didn't know it*), inhabited by the songs *that animate them*. Through them, the singers' voices are reincarnated and, in them, these *reincarnated* songs – which are also, at least to a certain extent, *clichés* – take on *an unexpected aspect*. As though, because of this astonishing film, it is now clear that there are only clichés which, when *displayed in a certain way* [*montés*], are liable to take on an *unexpected* aspect.[13]

This is surely Descartes' meaning when he writes:

> In the same way, we cannot write any word in which letters that are not in the alphabet are found, nor make any sentence except with terms that are in the dictionary: likewise a book, except with sentences that are to be found in others.[14]

Clichés which have been put into perspective take on, *in a certain context*, an aspect that Descartes calls their coherence – which we might also call their *assembly* [*montage*].

> But if the things that I say cohere so well together – and are so tightly bound (*connexa*) that each follows on from the others, then this will be the proof that I have no more borrowed these sentences from others than I have drawn the terms themselves from the dictionary.

In truth, these songs *fashion me* long before I cite them. I recite them without knowing that I am citing them, without realizing it. They are *interlaced* with the time of my consciousness, and without my being aware of it, except when, as in *Same Old Song*, I realize that in fact *every-one* knows the songs,[15] me included. And that, as such, this 'every' is a 'one' rather than a 'we': I belong to this neutral, impersonal, and yet so intimate, 'one'. This 'one' which is not, in the end, at least *not quite*, a 'we'. As though it were missing something. As though, in the time of temporal industrial objects, *we* were lacking.

How is it any different for the words used by Descartes? Words which he has not taken from the dictionary but which are there nevertheless – along with numerous phrases, cited as examples of usage, which we continually use in the mode of theme and variation.

12.   Grammar and sampling

It is a question of *grammar*, that is, of grammes, of the *specificities* of what I have referred to as ortho-grammes[16] – of which phonograms, videogrammes and DVDs are, like alphabetic orthography,[17] each particular instances. They are the bearers of *always original temporalities, which is to say syntheses (in the Kantian sense) conditioned by prostheses.*

It is this kind of alchemy, by which the 'one' *can* sometimes give an 'I' or a 'we', that is noted by the musician and singer Rodolphe Burger in his analysis of *sampling* and the practices of *house* musicians:

> It is as if someone in literature were to sell books that were catalogues of pre-*cuts*, with little cuts of Chateaubriand, in the same way as we have dictionaries of synonyms and rhymes.
>
> That's it. Technology gives access to what has already been processed, but what's interesting is that, in this context, people find a way of producing something new, even if this novelty can in no way be considered an original work.

But because these questions are posed by the technology of analogue reproduction just as much as by digital hyper-reproduction, albeit in a unique way each time, Resnais was able to make the following statement on the subject of *My American Uncle* – and we will return to these remarks:

> The idea of using excerpts from films was around from the first drafts of the screenplay. At one point we even considered making a film only using scenes drawn from the millions of films making up the history of cinema. Novels, the cinema and theatre all show how this might be done. With time and patience we might have succeeded. But in financial terms it would have been a crazy project.[18]

In *Same Old Song*,[19] the singers and their voices are cited, 'sampled', mixed and assembled – they are cut and set like stones on a ring. And, in a sense, *Same Old Song* follows on from *My American Uncle*, where the characters are inhabited by *excerpts from films*, but now with a particular focus on a specific aspect of the 'chanson populaire' (Claude François). In a similar way, although on a different register, as we will see, it also follows on from *Life is a Bed of Roses* [*La Vie est un Roman*], a film which was misunderstood at the time of its release. *Same Old Song* radicalizes the question that had already been opened in *Life is a Bed of Roses* on the subject of happiness and unhappiness and the *malaise* particular to an epoch that finds it *difficult to distinguish the two* – a question, THAT IS, of the *inscription* and *transmission* of memory, of *pedagogy*, of school and of knowledge. It does this by returning to a path already opened by *My American Uncle*, and by posing the question as a question of *ill-being*.

13. Ventriloquists (if not parrots and monkeys)

Resnais is an extraordinary DJ, and, because of this, he is able to make us not only listen with our ears, but also grasp [*entendre*] with our eyes. Even if he practises his *sampling* on, or rather *via*, imagery, it remains the case that song is a particular kind of industrial temporal object: it is an object that is *peculiar to an epoch*, peculiarly emblematic of this epoch in its perpetual 'suspension'. It is an essentially popular art form which reaches and affects *every* ear: we have heard [*entendu*] these songs, even if we never wanted to listen to them, as though through a kind of *mis-hearing* [*mal-entendu*]. In a similar way, directly or indirectly, television reaches every eye (and I would be increasingly tempted to say that it infects them). It is in this context that cinema has become, on the one hand, an art form for aficionados, for 'enlightened' groups, and, on the other, commercial *entertainment*, an extremely profitable symbolic industry targeting the hypermasses (those who are to be found at the hypermarkets).

All this, then, opens a number of questions peculiar to our epoch – or our *absence* of epoch – there where our epoch is *lacking*.

The characters do not speak. In is not in any case a matter of speaking, but neither do they sing: *it sings* [*ça chante*] in them, they are ventriloquized. They want to speak and it sings. These singing episodes always take place at key moments in the plot, and, through them, the characters in the film take on the character of the song they are singing (just as the characters in *My American Uncle* project excerpts of films *in their imaginations*): they *adopt*, in a certain sense, the spirit of the song. And we adopt, as we will see, the time, the hopes, the worries, and the feelings of the characters, and through them the time of these songs. *We find ourselves to be WITH THEM, feeling what is ultimately, and very paradoxically, a strange sense of relief in what we come to realize is their ill-being.*

Assumption and adoption, the heart of Resnais' cinema in *My American Uncle* and *Same Old Song*, are normal in the constitution of 'consciousnesses'. And this is why ultimately we must put this word prudently between inverted commas. 'Consciousness' is never constituted purely, simply and originally, in itself: it is always both a little bit monkey and a little bit parrot. It always inherits what it is not – this is its 'facticity'. And it has 'to be' this inheritance.

To *be* (Heidegger)? Or to *become* (Nietzsche)?

14.   Up against us

This initial situation of inheritance of a facticity is what I have formerly referred to as the *already-there*. This will once again be the focus of my analyses here, but as a *subject to be taken up* [*matière à monter*] – taken up *freely* in the *films projected by consciousnesses* as their *future*, and taken up into that faculty, at once higher and hidden, that is the Kantian *imagination*.

A free game without which there would be neither montage nor consciousness. Because what is a 'consciousness' that is not free, not free to say 'I' against every other 'I', against the 'we', against the 'one' – *against, right up against*, as Sacha Guitry says?[20]

You will say, therefore, that song here represents the normal situation of the soul and of consciousness, posing the question of liberty and the will, of the interplay of imagination and action, starting from the *prefabricated and passively received* facticity of a heteronomy preceding any other possibility. And you will be right – as long as it is understood that *here* it is a matter of a normal situation that is nevertheless singular, of *our* normality, which is ultimately fairly extra-ordinary. It is that of the epoch of *industrial* temporal objects that come to haunt our ears and eyes so that we no longer really know what to think about *who* we are – or *if* we *are*.

In question are the conditions of this prefabrication, which have evolved in a way that makes it difficult to be in place, in the already-there where we need 'to be'. This *already-there of our ill-being* is what is so well expressed by some of these songs. In certain respects these songs, accepted so *passively*, are, therefore, simultaneously, the *cause*, the *expression* and the possibility of *relief*, if not healing, of this ill-being.

Relief in the face of the trials inflicted on us by an *ill-becoming*.

In the course of the film we are surprised to find that we know so many songs that so many other people know as well: we are surprised, for example, that Alain Resnais knows and is interested in songs that we may never ourselves have taken an interest in before. We are surprised to discover that, in the end, we find them interesting as well, and that they have always affected us, perhaps more than we realized. In any case, we are surprised that they are interlaced with our consciousness, with its past flow, in the most secret and intimate way possible. And finally we are surprised, and a little disturbed, to find that WE LOVE THEM, and that perhaps we already *loved* them, without knowing it, without admitting it to ourselves (right at the start of the film I said to myself that I especially liked *Paroles* by Dalida and Alain Delon; and then, I realized that in the end I liked *all* the songs, most of which I had found so ridiculous before).

We encounter these songs in a cleverly constructed context which, in an *almost miraculous* way, lends them support while it is itself supported by them. And when we encounter these tunes – which we thought were so worn out, we who have become so *sceptical* and tired – in this context, it is *with the force of an indisputable poetic necessity*.

We take up the melodies and listen to the words from the depths of what used to be called *joy*.

Prayer: 'That my joy remain'.

15.   Beliefs, projections, scepticisms

Like us, the characters in the film know the songs, since they sing them. Straight away, then, we are close to them. The songs install between us a strange familiarity, about which it is difficult to know quite what to think, but which is clear and gentle, often very funny, sometimes poignant and sometimes overwhelming.

These recorded songs that we know so well and which remain *common to everyone and impersonal, animate* the *personality* of each character to such an extent that, at dramatic moments in the film, they sing these words *common to so many other consciousnesses*, rather than speak. And this surprises us, it makes us realize that we have never really *considered* the songs. It happens to the characters with such immediate *self-evidence* that we *believe* it, perhaps more than anything else that we could imagine. This dramatization, which is so spectacularly far from how we *think* we live in reality, reveals what *supports* that reality – but also, what is *insupportable* about that reality.

This film shows us a world where time has become industrialized, where the relationship with the past has become unclear, if not annulled – and because of this, Camille, a history student and the main character in the film, suffers.

> The film expresses nothing but ill-being. Alain Resnais has directed carefully, soberly and almost coldly. With a glacial aesthetic even. In what he shows of Paris – the nineteenth century (contemporary art is subject to mockery) – and in the (superb) sets, everything is marked by a contrast between the old and charming and the new and unliveable. No computer to establish the film in its epoch. We learn more about the Buttes-Chaumont Park than about today's fashionable districts. Everything that is worthless in our lives is described: the cynicism of mobiles, the idiocy of the remote control. And credit worries substitute for what is interesting (history, for example).[21]

I'm not sure that the *opposition* between old and new is as simple for Resnais as this cinema critic would have us believe. And if the film is not 'established in its epoch', it is perhaps because *this epoch is not quite an epoch*; because it is not *established*.

16. Creating disgust

Or it is a strange epoch, one that changes our understanding of what an epoch is. As an American advertising agency wrote in 1955, anticipating what, at the end of the century, would become a way of life across the globe:

> . . . what makes this country (North America) great is the creation of needs and desires, the creation of disgust for anything that is old and unfashionable.[22]

It is a fact, the creation of appetites is here the creation of disgust. Which then comes to affect the appetite created. And there is 'no more respect, none at all'.[23] Such a 'creation of needs', writes Vance Packard, 'appeals to the subconscious':

> The idea of appealing to the subconscious resulted in large part from the difficulties encountered by industries to make Americans buy what their factories were able to produce.[24]

The most effective instruments in the creation of disgust for the old and unfashionable, and in the supposedly correlative desire for the *novel* [*neuf*] – if not the *new* [*nouveau*] – which is to say in the creation of needs corresponding to the interests of industrial development, are the systems of mass media and the cultural industries. These are the vehicles of the advertising industry and constitute a distribution system for industrial temporal objects, providing a *means of access to the time of consciousnesses*, which is increasingly subjected to systematic exploitation.

After the Second World War, *advertising* began to *target* consciousness as an available (but not inexhaustible) resource, which is to say as merchandise. This is even the precondition for 'development'. And in this *total mobilization of that which produces mobility* as such, namely *motivations* (in the 1950s Packard analysed in detail the emergence of MR or 'motivational research'), *industrial temporal objects are privileged instruments*, as they intertwine ideally and massively with the *time of consciousnesses*.

And it is this that would intensify frighteningly in the coming years, as is suggested by B. Joseph Pine and James Gilmore, for whom:

> in the emerging Experience Economy, companies must realize that they make memories, not goods.[25]

The outdated, the old and the *ageing*, are staged by Resnais as being in confrontation not so much with modernity as with modernity's *lack*, with the *nothing* that this modernity would ultimately become *through exhaustion of the 'consciousness of modernity'*. It is a time about which we do not know what we *should* think – like we do not know what to think of a 'modern' sculpture, pejoratively referred to as a 'pile of plates' by a character in the film, who is himself rather vulgar. Common judgement is suspended, unable to decide.

Via songs which, at great depth and secrecy, constitute the already-there, Resnais stages simultaneously:

- the fact that this already-there has become *structurally outdated*;
- the resulting *ill-being*, particularly for the *historian* Camille;
- and *song's durability*, its extraordinary structuring *power* [*pouvoir*], the extent to which it is *known, as compared to the weakness of sculpture – the representative of fine art*.

The kind of popular song that predominates here is certainly shown to constitute a foundation for what is sometimes called the 'social bond'. And yet, while recorded song has clearly configured a new kind of *we*, the *we* in question is *dejected and suffering* – suffering and *ashamed* of its *becoming-one*. The shame of being a man.

17. Love Paris

The film begins in Paris in 1945 with a threat of catastrophe interrupted by this song:

J'ai deux amours, mon pays et Paris . . .[26]

The singer is General von Choltitz who, in this way, disobeys an order he has just received from Hitler to blow up Paris.

The interruption of the threat by the song is a kind of miracle.

The destruction of Paris would have meant the erasure of an accumulation of pasts without equivalent in the world. An accumulation that is visible and readable in the buildings, in the names of streets, in gardens and in the squares and parks with their statues. It would have meant the end of a time which, like nowhere else, is *perhaps* still possible here, and which so many visitors and tourists, seen throughout the course of the film, come to experience.

The story [*historie*] begins, therefore, with History [*Histoire*], which also introduces Camille: historian and the heroine of the film. I have already underlined that, in *Same Old Song*, we who 'know' the songs sung by the characters are *necessarily a public living in France*. General von Choltitz, himself living in France, ultimately succumbs to the 'charms of Paris' to the point where this *place* carries more weight, more *authority* and *force*, than the dictator, the supreme leader of the German armed forces. One way or another, this German saved Paris. Von Choltitz loved Paris.

Hitler's order was a threat to an impressive concretization of what I have referred to as epiphylogenesis[27] – that store of memory that is particular to a unique life form – the human – and that is also the 'life of the spirit'. It is a matter of memory retained in things. From diaries to buildings, and passing by books, fetishes and registries of all kinds – including films and recorded songs. Paris is the example *par excellence*, and in its fullest dimension, of this epiphylogenetic structuring of *lived space – lived to the extent that it produces events*. Which is only *liveable* as such. And which, as such, affects its inhabitants as well as its visitors, *inhabiting*, in a certain way, *their spirit*.

Epiphylogenesis, time spaced and space temporalized, is the sedimentary store of events among which we live without knowing it. It is a memory that is transmitted down the generations (which haunt and *spiritualize* each other). Being spatialized it is exteriorized and retained *in the facticity of the non-living* – protected from the *fragility* of the living.

18.   Epiphylogenesis and tertiary retentions

Epiphylogenesis is the *process of production* of what I call tertiary *retentions*, in order to distinguish them from primary and secondary retentions as defined by Husserl. Let us look once more at the melody, the first temporal object studied by Husserl, so as to understand what is going on here – I recall, in summary, the analyses already undertaken in *Cinematic Time and the Question of Malaise*.

In the 'now' of a melody, in the present moment of a musical object in flux, the present note can only be a note – and not simply a sound – *to the extent that it retains in itself the preceding note* and that in the preceding note the note that preceded it is *still present*, which retains in turn the preceding note, etc. This *primary retention*, which *belongs to the present* of *perception*, must not be confused with *secondary retention*, which is the melody I might have heard yesterday, for example, which I am able to listen to again *in imagination* through the play of memory, and which constitutes the *past* of my consciousness. You must not confuse, says Husserl, perception (primary retention) with imagination (secondary retention). Before the invention of the phonograph it was absolutely impossible to listen to the *same* melody twice. But, with the appearance of the phonogram, which is itself what I have referred to as a 'tertiary retention' (a prosthesis, memory exteriorized), the identical repetition of the same temporal object has become possible. And this enables us to understand better the processes of retention. Because, as a result:

– when the same temporal *object* occurs twice in a row it produces two *different* temporal *phenomena*, meaning that primary retentions vary from one phenomenon to the next: the retentions from the first time of listening play, when they have become secondary, a selective role for the primary retentions of the second time of listening. This is true in general, but the phonogram, as tertiary retention, makes it clear; repetition produces difference;

– on the other hand, temporal objects that have become tertiary, which is to say recorded (the phonogram, but also films and radio and television shows), are time materialized and they organize the relationship between primary and secondary retentions in general, allowing in certain respects for their control. And difference can be annulled by tertiary retentions just as much as it can be intensified by them: repetition can lead to indifference.

All this is a question of desires and drives, and of the compulsion to repeat. Eros and Thanatos have a whole arsenal with which to oppose each other, but more assuredly, and above all, with which to *compose*. Starting with songs.

19. Miracle and concern

Epiphylogenesis, of which the phonogram is a unique example, is the *sedimentary deposit* left by the process of production of tertiary retentions of all kinds, and it is here that the arsenal is constituted. But, while it is protected by its exteriority, *material* epiphylogenetic memory can also be *destroyed forever*. This is what does not happen to Paris – what is miraculously avoided – and this is also the 'miracle' that is song.

The inhabitation of the General's mind by Paris is equal to the weight on his spirit, or consciousness, of tertiary retentions. Epiphylogenesis is both the process of production and the resultant system of these retentions. But the film demonstrates the authority that objectivized retentions of another kind have assumed, not only over the General, but *over us* as well: *recorded songs*. And this authority is the *source* of a discomfort that proves to be a true ill-being.

Epiphylogenesis, and the retentions that constitute it as a system, are the condition for the constitution of a *we*. This *we* – inhabited, therefore, by the space it inhabits – is now also inhabited, as it already was in 1945, by the songs that circulate in this space. Politics is first and foremost the politics of these 'tertiary retentions'. This is the deep meaning of Hitler's destructive will which, we know only too well, was very attentive to the question of traces: involving as it did the annihilation of a retentional apparatus of which Paris formed only a part.

But it is in the direction of an *obliteration*, if not of Paris then at least of a particular *view* of Paris, that Alain Resnais' modern drama leads us.

You have to see [*voir*] Paris. And not only see it but know it [*savoir*]. It is in this way that we are introduced to Camille, tour guide and history student. At the beginning of the story she is in the process of finishing a thesis on 'the farmer knights of Lake Paladru in the year 1000'. The second sequence of the film takes place on Rue de Rivoli outside the building occupied by the German commander, and it is Camille who explains to the tourists and to us as viewers the meaning of the preceding scene, and that Paris might well have been blown up.

But, what is retained in the buildings and the monuments of this city is perhaps, even *certainly*, even *necessarily*, *always under threat*. Such is Camille's concern, which will become her malaise, and result in her collapse.

20.   Camille and history

Camille is a historian, but she is also a tour guide: she talks about Paris – with its monuments, its historic places and its parks – to tourists, pensioners and the unemployed. Her sister Odile is almost her opposite. She is a modern, strong-minded woman in a position of responsibility in a business, who dreams of owning a new-build apartment with magnificent views over Paris.

As opposed to Odile, who sings every time she appears on the screen, Camille hardly ever sings: only twice when she falls in love with a hateful character called Marc (who Odile finds cute: 'That Marc is so cute!'). Camille sings twice and then she *loses her voice*: she sinks into depression.

She falls in love and then, almost immediately, she 'defends' her thesis. It is on the day of this defence that she experiences her first feelings of malaise. She suffocates. This scene is a turning point in the film. Where there was comedy, charm and lightness, there are lies, illnesses and anxieties. Everything pivots for the first time in the film during the defence of this thesis – a thesis which every-one makes fun of to a certain extent (except her father and her sister, Odile – who says that Camille is 'the gifted one in the family').

'A thesis on what?' asks one of Odile's friends called Nicolas after hearing Camille state the 'subject' ('farmer knights of Lake Paladru in the year 1000'). 'On . . . nothing!' replies Camille.

> Nicolas – Is anyone interested in this . . .?
> Camille – No, no one!
> Nicolas – Then why did you choose the subject?
> Camille – To give the morons something to talk about.

'It's always the same,' Camille then says to Odile, 'they ask you what it's about and then they snigger.' When she hears that the university has decided to publish her thesis, the news upsets her: 'Are there more than fifteen people who would be interested in this subject?' she asks despondently. Every time she has to speak about the thesis, instead of furnishing her the pleasure of refined conversation, it gives rise to an idle chit-chat which bears witness to the misery of the time and the vanity of all desire for knowledge, as well as any 'learned' position (*thesis*) or attitude. It bears witness to the liquidation of any 'extended' timeframe by the present time, to the vacuity of historical memory properly speaking, and, finally, to the *inanity* of the university institution in its totality. As though, despite von Choltitz's refusal, Paris and all the knowledge it held had finally burned.

There is no doubt that these scenes express Resnais' kindly, almost touching, irony with regard to university 'research'. And yet, you get the feeling that they are also about Resnais' irony with regard to himself, and that what haunts Camille is also what *obsesses* Resnais – as though Camille were a cover for Alain Resnais and his own distress. This is illustrated by the furtive *apparition* of the knights of the year 1000 to Camille in an extremely short shot coming just after the declaration of her malaise (which will become her depression). These knights and the lake where they live, which are properly speaking a *hallucination*, come in the quasi-return of a scene constituting the *underground*, and in a sense 'epiphylogenetic', stratum of *Life is a Bed of Roses* (like a citation of Resnais by Resnais, a memory stratum of the character Alain Resnais surreptitiously entering on scene in his own film).

Camille sees these knights when she leaves her sister Odile chatting with Marc Duveyrier in a luxury hotel as she goes down to the toilets. Leaves her, that is, with her cretin of a fiancé who is so different from her and who, so attached to the present, so modern, with so few qualms and so little soul, is making her increasingly unwell. It is 'a site that has remained completely intact, it is a snapshot of daily life in the Middle Ages', she says of Lake Paladru, at the same time sensing the pointlessness of the thesis. This is also a *doubt with respect to contemporary knowledge*, just as we detect everywhere a *suspicion with respect to art*, even if this doubt and this suspicion are not the same: the knowledge in doubt is not that of industrial science (but is this still knowledge, is it *sapid*?), it is the old, the ancient, the unfashionable. While, erected in a recently re-urbanized square in a regenerated area of the city, the sculpture held to ridicule is contemporary ('I quite like it', says Simon, who loves Odile who loves, or thinks she loves, Marc).

21. Appearances, lies, fictions

'I couldn't care less!
What?
Who then? you should ask! Thus spoke Dionysus.'

After the defence, Camille doubts *everything*.
   'I couldn't care less about my thesis', she says to Simon when, after having fallen in love with Marc, and, victim to her second malaise, she begins to kid herself – which makes her sing:

> I couldn't care less
> Whatever might be
> I couldn't care less
> I have my love with me
> It's pretty plain
> Think what they dare
> It's all the same
> I don't care. (Edith Piaf)[28]

Camille will soon, however, sink into depression,[29] and, all of a sudden, all the characters find themselves in a situation of disarray and disorientation with regard to the spirit of an insipid age. And soon the appearances, which concealed their deeper motivations from the eyes of the characters, will be torn away – with the exception of Marc, who is nothing but a liar. This tearing away of appearances constitutes the last part of the film, which begins the moment that Jane Birkin comes on scene.

Jane plays Jeanne, the wife of Nicolas, a character affected physically by his psychological states – melancholia, hypochondria and a degree of mythomania. It is when she is talking things through with her husband that Jeanne, a victim of her partner's malaise, sings *What?*

But is it not rather Jane who sings *What?* Is it not rather *to Serge* that this song is addressed – to Gainsbourg who also wrote it and who is now dead?

It is a song which, on this occasion, is not mimed but sung by the singer who created it and who, as an actress, also has a role in Alain Resnais' film. An actress who brings a part of her life to the film along with her fascinating skin, filmed magnificently in close-up, and which one cannot help admiring. This song is a pivot: with it a whole series of revelations is set off.

The finale is *triggered* when Jeanne sings *What?* because, unlike the other characters, Jeanne is *almost* her own character: she sings *her* song, she is not ventriloquized by a borrowed song, she is not inhabited by impersonal words, it is *her* expressing herself.

The character played by Jane Birkin is fictional and, singing her song so as to enact this fiction, the *character* is haunted by the *life* of the star, the life of the *singer* who is *also* the *actress*.

Of course, we hear *What?* as though Jane were playing herself. But, at the same time, this song here communicates Jeanne's malaise, and not only Jane's past. It communicates the malaise she feels in her relationship with Nicolas, her husband in the film, who 'never stops fooling himself'. The character in the film and the character of the actress (and singer) are *superimposed* in an extraordinary way. This scene between Jeanne and Nicolas necessarily 'sticks' to, strangely and *indiscreetly* adheres to, if I may put it like this, an overwhelming truth. To what we imagine Jane Birkin must be thinking when she sings *What?*, to her own life, to her relationship with a man we think she must have loved, a man we know: another singer, Serge Gainsbourg, whose ghost we cannot help projecting onto the screen.

This is only possible because Jane Birkin, who plays herself without really doing so, is in a triple fiction, so fictitious and complex that it becomes *sublimely true*:

- the fiction of the character that she is playing;
- the fiction of this game, since she is not really playing – 'this isn't a game' a child might say;
- the fiction that what she is singing, her song, is only a song – a fiction – which seems to be addressed to Gainsbourg when it was in fact written by him who is now dead.

This creates a sumptuous tissue of appearances, which is nothing but a shadow theatre and a confusion of ghosts.

22.   Good = bad

But these appearances save. Staged in this way and made to 'cohere', as Descartes would have said, they 'save phenomena'. Singing with her familiar English accent, Jane Birkin perhaps unintentionally reverses the situation, just as von Choltitz saves Paris. The songs that we know [que l'*on* conaît] are always sung in French even if idiomatically marked, but it is two resident *foreigners* who are the true heroes of the film – if by this we mean saviours, heroic figures of deliverance.

The characters are all, to a degree, consumed by melancholy or anxiety, and all, to a degree, victims of denial. All, that is, except for Simon, who falls in love with Camille, a self-confessed long-term depressive, and Marc, with whom Camille falls in love, who has no trace of depression or anxiety. Marc is *modern*, in a way that Odile would like to be – much more modern than Odile who is too troubled by scruples and remorse. Marc has no qualms, he is cynical, self-interested, dishonest and a liar: he embodies a good deal of that which engenders melancholy in the other characters, precisely because he is very 'modern'. His lie is revealed at the end of the film, at the same time as the other characters confess to each other and to themselves, the basis of their ill-being. 'Everything you've said, everything you've described, is exactly the same for me', Nicolas says to Camille, who is describing her 'symptoms'. Then he says to Simon:

I was wrong about Camille. She's a good girl. I didn't know that she was in a bad way like that.

To be in a 'bad' way is 'good'.

Even Marc will end up admitting that he is 'unloved' ['*malaimé*'], that 'deep down he is in despair' ['*a un "désespoir au fond de" lui*'] (Claude François). And Nicolas ends up phoning Jeanne in England to talk things over with her:

> Something has turned ugly
> And it's broken,
> I don't want you to go. (Michel Jonas)[30]

Speaking to Camille about depression, a subject he knows well, Simon says:

> You well know
> It's nothing
> Time passes
> And it comes back. (Julien Clerc)[31]

And Claude, Odile's husband, follows on with Claude François:

> It goes and it comes
> Made up of little nothings
> Sings and dances with itself
> It comes back and holds back
> Like a pop song . . .[32]

In the end it is Marc who sings last with *Blues de blanc* by Eddy Mitchell.

The *blues*.

These final minutes when the characters articulate in all manner of ways the *sickness from which they suffer*, are *for us* a moment of *great well-being*. Phew! It's *said*. It's out. *Our* illness has been articulated.

23. 'Me neither . . .'

In *What?*, Jane, or Jeanne, sings:

You'd rather die than give up.[33]

After which Nicolas sings:

> It was the last show
> It was the last sequence
> And the curtain on the screen
> Has fallen. (Eddy Mitchell)[34]

It is from *What?* onwards that it will become possible to 'verbal-ize', as they say, the ill-being – still through song. The songs then get going again, in particular those of Claude François, but now with a different tonality. They begin to soar, ultimately following on from each other without interruption and carrying us into a kind of joyous intoxication. At the beginning of this almost tragic finale, of this cathartic process, this liberating explosion, all of the characters, addressing themselves to Camille, sing together these words from the band Téléphone:

> That, that's you all over!
> That's clear,
> That, that's you all over!
> That's clear, that it's you!
> That's clear, that it's you![35]

In order to prepare us for this grandiose scene, for this celebra-tion, Resnais plays on the fact that, one way or another, we all know Jane Birkin's song (as Fellini had done with Anita Ekberg in *Interview*). His editing in the film animates a part of us, it moves us. And, because it is here sung by Jane Birkin herself, we project a situation that is exceptional FOR US. Jane Birkin tells us about something from her own life and, in all likelihood, from her love life with Serge Gainsbourg – at least, we cannot not think this when we listen to her. Because, while it is a love song like so many others, this is about an affair that began *publicly* during an erotic year in 1969, when it was there to hear on any radio:

> Serge Gainsbourg:
> I come, I go and I come,
> Between your loins,
> I go and I come,
> Between your loins,

And I
hold
back . . .[36]

Jane Birkin:
I love you,
Yes I love you . . .[37]

Whether we like it or not, we have all known this couple, Serge Gainsbourg and Jane Birkin – we, the *inhabitants of France at the end of the twentieth century*. One year after 1968. In a way we are part of the family. This is our scrapbook.

24. Blocked view

At the end we find out that the view over Paris from the apartment bought by Odile and Claude will be blocked by a new building, and that Marc Duveyrier, who is Camille's fiancé and the modern estate agent who sold the apartment to Odile, lied to her. It is as though Paris were condemned to disappear, or Odile to lose her sight, and her life. I will come back to this blindness as it relates to the film *Tiresia*.[38]

In this film so full of ambiguities, it is recorded song and its subtle exploration through cinema that provides the principal subject and the tension. Through it 'the emotion and the reason of the spectator come together in process', as Eisenstein would say. Recorded song is here simultaneously the cause of ill-being, the industrialization of appearances, and the possibility of deliverance – its expression and its nurturing revelation.

> The latest Resnais is, paradoxically, a sad film from which you come out happy . . . What's that about?
> Funny, full of humour, Resnais's film leaves a sweet feeling of euphoria, and an impression of wellbeing. But the film speaks of nothing but ill-being.

This is what Aristotle would have called *catharsis* – a concept that belongs to a political thinking of aesthetics.

But, if it is true that the ill-being staged by this film stems from the ruin of primordial narcissism, and is, in this sense, shared by the characters of the film, the viewers, the French voters of the election of 21 April 2002, as well as Richard Durn[39] and so many others the world over who are humiliated and offended, then the most important political question – maybe the only one, if ever a question can still be political – is that of the *aesthetics of the we*. In the age of the industrial exploitation of the times of consciousness and of spirit, the age of the lack of age, as though *we* were lacking . . .

III

Allegory of the Anthill[1]
The Loss of Individuation in the Hyper-industrial Age

It does not seem as though any influence could induce a man to change his nature into a termite's.

Sigmund Freud

25. Forewarning

I am going to try to talk to you about the individual in the contemporary age, an age I will qualify as hyper-industrial. And I will do so starting from the concept of individuation developed by Simondon – where individuation is conceived as a *process* which is always *both psychic and collective* – where *I* and *we* are therefore two aspects of the same process, and where the *difference* between them is also the *dynamic* of the process.

Now, it is a principle for Simondon that to *say* individuation, which is to *know* it as an *I* addressing a *we*, is to *individuate* it. It is, in other words, to pursue it and, in this way, to alter it, to make it become or trans-form it. Jean-François Lyotard, the philosopher of 'postmodernity', would perhaps have said: to *per-form* or *work-through* [*per-laborer*] it. But I don't think he was aware of Simondon. If to know individuation is always to transform it, then the question arises as to the very possibility of knowing it. To what extent can my discourse now be understood in terms of knowledge? Simondon's response is clear: you *cannot know individuation*. What kind of discourse is this then?

Whether or not it is accorded a 'cognitive' status, this discourse belongs to a particular rationality where, *saying* (philosophically) individuation, I *individuate* it, or I *singularize* it – necessarily singularizing *myself* at the same time. Saying it is *doing* it. It is essentially a kind of performativity, in Austin's sense, where I *am involved with the object* I describe: I am *engaged*. The individuation in which I participate in this way is not therefore mine alone: according to Simondon's theory it is always already that of a group to which I address myself – and to which I belong precisely through my address, through the fact that *with* this address I *participate* in its individuation.

This group is you, and you and me constitute a *we*. And all this means that what I have to say will be *political* – and much more performative than it is cognitive. This is what I wanted to warn you about as we begin.

26. Disfiguration of the individual and loss of individuation in the hyper-industrial age

By *modernity* I mean that which characterizes *industrial* society. Which is why, if ever it were necessary to speak of *hyper-modernity* (which would, however, require a minute and scrupulous critique of the concept of post-modernity, where everything need not be discarded),[2] this could only be in the same sense as we speak of that which characterizes *hyper-industrial* society – the very opposite of what we have thought it possible to refer to as 'post-industrial' society, which has never been anything but a chimera. And the same goes, by and large, and for this same reason, for the 'post-modern'.

The first lines of *The Postmodern Condition* take it for granted that we have passed into the post-industrial age, and in this way take up unproblematically Alain Touraine's thesis – a thesis which on the contrary seems to me completely inadmissible, and which for a number of years has served as a block to any political thought. Lyotard writes:

> Our working hypothesis is that the status of knowledge is altered as societies enter what is known as the postindustrial age and cultures enter what is known as the postmodern age.[3]

And a note refers here to various works on the coming of the post-industrial age, in particular *The Post-Industrial Society* by Alain Touraine.

I argue to the contrary that we have not left modernity because more than ever we are experiencing the *industrialization of all things*. It is clearly possible to put forward another definition of modernity where it is not seen simply as the becoming-industrial of society. In this case we would open different perspectives on the question of a possible 'hyper-modernity'. One could, for example, say that modernity refers to a society where *calculation* has come to rule through the project of *mathesis universalis* and the domination of nature by technics: this is the Heideggerian definition. Or again, one could characterize modernity by way of capitalism as the advent of the bourgeoisie, realized in the industrialization of society. This is the Marxian definition. There is also the definition of control societies, which is clearly related to these two thoughts.

The advent of calculation and capitalism are in fact aspects of the same development, which is *realized* as a decisive historical situation by the industrial revolution, thus establishing an epoch properly speaking. And this is what needs to be taken into account. Not so as to suggest that this historical situation has come to an end (that we are in the post-industrial, and therefore the post-modern, epoch), but because, *on the contrary*, we believe that it is *becoming more extensive, more intensive and more complex*. With the entry into the bio-digital age we encounter a new set of issues compared to the era of the thermal and electric machine – essentially characterizing what Deleuze calls control societies.

The Heideggerian and Marxian characterizations of modernity complement my own. And I believe that the Deleuzian question of control is also to be found in this same vein (this is why Deleuze can call himself a Marxist[4] while at the same time arguing that Heidegger and Foucault[5] are the two thinkers who have changed the thought of the twentieth century. Heidegger being for that matter one of the key interlocutors in *Difference and Repetition*). In this way we will see that the hyper-industrial age can be characterized *as an extension of calculation beyond the sphere of production along with a correlative extension of industrial domains*. This is what is now commonly called the third industrial revolution, and we will see that this generalized computation brings calculation *fully* into the characteristic mechanisms of what Simondon calls *psychic and collective individuation*. In other words, hyper-industrialization brings about a new figure of the individual. But, and this is the paradox of my title, it is a *figure of the individual that finds itself disfigured* insomuch as the hyper-industrial generalization of calculation *creates an obstacle* to the *processes of individuation*, which alone make the individual possible.

Thus a new form of capitalism develops (one which Rifkin calls cultural), where it is not the entrepreneur-producer who makes the law, but rather marketing in its *control of the temporalities* of consciousnesses and bodies through the mechanization of daily life. A control that takes place therefore by way of all those *mechanical things* which, beyond cars and washing machines, include televisions, mobile telephones, electronic diaries, computers and *home cinemas*. Things that are structured on retentional apparatuses, but also on biotechnological apparatuses, which establish hyper-industrial biopower and which constitute the general *organological horizon* with, for, against and in which it is necessary to struggle – for the benefit of individual singularities – to the extent that *we* are concerned and want to remain a *we*.

27. Individual and machine

Simondon characterizes modernity by way of the industrial *machine* and as the appearance of a *new kind of individual*. But this is a *technical individual*: the machine itself. Before the machines, we read in *On the Mode of Existence of Technical Objects*,[6] man was a *tool carrier*, and he was himself the technical *individual*. In the modern-industrial era, it is the *machines* that are the tool carriers – and man is *no longer* the technical individual; he has become either their servant (worker), or their assembler (engineer or manager).

Two questions arise here:

1. What is the *place of the machine* in individuation *today* – is it possible to speak of a *hyper-industrial mechanical*

individuation, constitutive of a psychic and collective individuation that we would, for this reason, call *hyper-modern?*
2. According to Simondon's analysis, there are 'technical individuals' that are machines: what does this mean in general for the thought of the human individual, and how do these technical individuals affect the individual of the hyper-industrial age?

First element of a general response: according to Simondon, industrial society constitutes, from the perspective of work, a *loss of individuation. The worker is no longer a technical individual*[7] *because the machine has formalized his actions. In this way he becomes proletarian* – having been replaced by the machine which has become the technological individual and to which he is nothing but a servant. This 'nothing but' is experienced, Simondon says, as a humiliation – an aspect of the discontent that Freud sought to think.

The mechanical formalization of the actions of the worker results from an *analysis* followed by a *synthesis* – and it is produced as an *artefact* by *technoscience. Let us note in passing that a formalization of this kind is a sort of grammatization* – in Sylvain Auroux's sense of the term:[8] analysis as *discretization of the continuous.* I will come back to this crucial point later so as to demonstrate that grammatization (thought in another way by Jacques Derrida, following Leroi-Gourhan) is the very condition of constitution for the Abrahamic people of the Book, for the 'apparatus' of the Greek city-state as analysed by Michel Foucault, and ultimately *for the process of Western individuation in its entirety.*

There is a question here as to whether biodigital hyper-industrial technology *follows* from or *completes* this process of Western individuation – as the now globalized epoch of the process of individuation of terrestrial technical life (called human). For my part, I maintain that the current stage of grammatization has brought us to the limit of individuation, to a loss of individuation *at the point of completion* of the process of psychic and collective individuation in general. An impossible limit which can only lead to a reversal, and, in this sense, a 'revolution' – that is to say, the closure of one cycle establishing at its limit a completely different [*tout autre*] cycle: the cycle of the completely different [*tout-autre*] in the whirlwind of what is ultimately a spiral (which today appears to be a 'downward' spiral [*spiral 'infernale'*]).

Whatever the case may be, we will see that a *process of grammatization* supports the process of political individuation such that it is punctuated by a *succession of losses of individuation*. The loss of individuation characteristic of the hyper-industrial age would thus be a *limit-case*. What I referred to above as the disfiguration of the contemporary hyper-industrial individual would therefore represent a new stage, however unusual, in the loss of individuation, which is *related to a new stage in the history of machines and therefore of technoscience, and which also represents a new stage in the process of grammatization.*

In order to understand the present condition of individuation, it is necessary to analyse earlier conditions, going back well before modernity: I will therefore have to speak to you about *the psychic and collective individuation of Western society over the long term*, and in such a way that it is precisely *connected to the process of grammatization*. But in order to do this, I will first need to make a few remarks on Simondon's understanding of individuation, supplementing these with certain results from my own work.

28.   Individuation and retentional apparatuses: the three strands of individuation

In *Cinematic Time* I set out that:

1. The *I*, as *psychic individual*, cannot be thought except to the extent that it belongs to a *we*, which is a *collective individual*: the *I* constitutes itself through the adoption of a collective history, which it inherits and with which a plurality of *I*s identify.
2. This inheritance is an adoption in the sense that, as the grandson of German immigrants, I can identify with a past which is not that of my ancestors, but which I can nevertheless make my own; this process of adoption is thus structurally artificial.
3. An *I* is essentially a *process* and not a state, and this process is an *in-dividuation* (this is the process of psychic

individuation) in that it is a *tendency* to becoming-one, which is to say *in-divisible*.

4. This tendency *never comes to a conclusion* because it encounters a *counter-tendency* with which it enters into a *metastable* equilibrium – and it is necessary to underline here that the Freudian theory of drives is particularly close to this conception of the dynamic of individuation, as is the thought of Empedocles and that of Nietzsche.

5. A *we* is also this kind of process (this is the process of collective individuation), the individuation of the *I* being always inscribed in that of the *we*, while, inversely, the individuation of the *we* only takes place through the conflicting individuations of the *I*s that compose it.

6. The *I* and the *we* are bound in individuation by the *pre-individual milieu*, with its positive conditions of effectiveness coming from what I have called *retentional apparatuses*. These apparatuses are supported by the technical milieu which is the condition for the encounter of the *I* and the *we*: the individuation of the *I* and the *we* is, in this sense, also the individuation of a *technical system* (something Simondon strangely didn't see).

7. The technical system is an apparatus which plays a particular role (and in which every object is held: a technical object only exists as *arranged* with other objects in the midst of such an apparatus – this is what Simondon called the 'technical ensemble'); the gun and, more generally, the technical-becoming with which it is in system are the constitutive possibilities of a disciplinary society in Foucault.[9]

8. The technical system also supports the constitutive possibility of retentional apparatuses, which are born of the process of grammatization taking place in the midst of the process of individuation of the technical system. And these retentional apparatuses condition the organization of the individuation of the *I* with the individuation of the *we* in a single process of *psychic, collective and technical*[10] individuation (where *grammatization* is a *sub-system of technics*). A process which therefore comprises *three strands*, each one dividing itself into processual sub-ensembles (in individuating itself, for example, the technical system also individuates its mnemotechnical and mnemotechnological systems).

29. Individuation as selection

As we have already seen,[11] an *I* is also a consciousness consisting of a temporal *flux* of *primary retentions*. The primary retention is what consciousness *retains* in the *now* of the flux that constitutes it: for example, the note that resonates is a note that is present to my consciousness as the passage of a melody, where the preceding note is not absent, but very much present, because maintained in and by the now, even though, as Husserl says, it has just passed. *My conscious life is essentially made up of such retentions*, which can be just as much phenomena that I *receive* as ones that I *produce* (a melody that I *play* or *hear*, a sentence that I *utter* or *hear*, a sequence of actions that I *accomplish* or that I *undergo*, etc.). Listening to me (or reading me), for example, you 'primarily retain' the words that are constitutive of sentences and that form the now of my discourse.

But *these retentions are selections*: you do not retain *everything* that could be retained.[12] In the flux of what appears to your consciousness, you make selections which are personal retentions; these selections are made through *the filters of secondary retentions* which are held in your memory and which constitute your experience. And I argue that conscious life consists of such an organization of primary retentions (R1), filtered by secondary retentions (R2), with the relations of primary retentions and secondary retentions ultimately determined by what I call tertiary retentions (R3) – these R3 relating just as much to technical individuation as to the process of grammatization which traverses it.

These interactions can be written as follows:

$$R3\,(R2\,(R1))$$

But since R1 is in fact always a selection, we should write it S1:

$$R3\,(R2\,(R1 = S1))$$

Or even:

$$((S1 = R1) = f\,(R2)) = f\,(R3)$$

Clearly, such a flux should not be thought of as an even line. It is less a line than a tissue or a weave – what I have referred to as my temporal *fabric* – such that certain *motifs* and *designs* are delineated there. The primary retention is here also the recurrence, the return, the refrain and the *haunting* [*revenance*] of that which persists. Ultimately the flux is a whirling spiral where events may take place; the eating of a Madeleine, for example. And one could demonstrate that a primary selection is the repetition of a secondary retention in what is primarily retained from what has happened. But also, for the same reason and at the same time:

- *that there is only repetition* (everything is the reactivation of a secondary retention, that is, its repetition);
- *that there is never repetition* (nothing ever happens again in an identical way: the repetition of the same temporal object always produces two different phenomena).

In any case, tertiary retentions result from what I call the epiphylogenetic situation of the *genre*, constituting the technical life that corresponds to what we also call the human species – which, being originally constituted by its prostheticity, has at its disposal a third, technical memory, which is neither genetic nor epigenetic.[13] And this is why it is not enough to call it a species. The epiphylogenetic milieu, as the *gathering of tertiary retentions*, constitutes the *support* of the pre-individual milieu allowing for the individuation of the genre.[14] The tertiary retentions form *retentional apparatuses* which define different epochs of epiphylogenesis.[15] And the different retentional apparatuses call for different criteriologies: how these are defined is subject to conflict.[16]

30.   A brief history of Western individuation

(a)   Grammatization

In the West, *the theatre of this conflict is the process of grammatization.* And this operational theatre has seen a long war of spirits [*esprits*] where *sym-bols* and *dia-bols* are constantly created to feed, *in the play of a tendency with its constitutive*[17] *and in principle*[18] *irreducible counter-tendency*, the *metabolism* of Western psychic and collective individuation.

According to Sylvain Auroux, the alphabet constitutes a *process of grammatization* (a *becoming-letter* of sound and word) which precedes all logic and all grammar, all science of language and all science in general, and which is the *techno-logical condition* (in the sense that it is always already both technical and logical)[19] of all knowledge, which begins with its exteriorization. The *third industrial revolution*, which is the generalization of informational technologies and the resulting redefinition of knowledge, belongs to this process of grammatization – and more precisely to the *third technological revolution of grammatization*, the second, according to Sylvain Auroux, being the printing revolution.

In fact, I am not exactly of the same view as Auroux here. He limits it to the grammatization of language, when today bodies as well, with the temporal sequences of gestures (including the voice) and movements (in the first place as cinemato-graphy),[20] are subject to grammatization through sound and image. What's more, this third revolution of grammatization begins in the nineteenth century, but in order to evaluate it one must analyse the *new technologies of discretization* that come into existence with programmable machines and information in the form of data, along with analogue techniques for recording sounds and images.

For Auroux, to grammatize means to discretize in order to isolate grammes, or the finite number of components forming a system. Even though it is not discrete, the analogical allows for repetitions which open a new comprehension of grammes: this is why Benjamin saw in cinema an extension of apperception, where analogical technologies lend themselves to editing and mixing and the constitution of elements forming an analytical system. It is in this way that they belong to grammatization.

This should not be confused with grammaticalization: grammatization precedes grammatical theory. Sylvain Auroux is interested in the historical conditions of access to the power of grammatization, and he shows beyond doubt that the *technical* practice of grammatization, bound up with different utilitarian concerns, precedes significantly the theories it conditions and makes possible. In short, it is not the grammarians who invent grammatization, but grammatization, as an *essentially technical* occurrence, which produces the grammarians – and what I will happily call the 'diagrammatologies' that analyse them *at second remove* [*dans un second après-coup*].

In the history of the process of Western psychic and collective individuation, grammatization, as technical individuation, is a weapon in the *control of idioms*, and, through them, of spirits [*esprits*], or retentional activity: the grammatization of an idiom is its transformation (individuation). It is never the case that the process of describing an idiom by grammatization leaves that idiom intact, including, and above all, when it results in a grammatical theory – the *general grammar* coming from the grammars of Lancelot, for example, which although it was Jansenist, lent support to the Jesuit missionaries in their colonization of spirits [*esprits*]. Sylvain Auroux gives as an example the Ma grammar, the first Chinese grammar he says, which succeeded in projecting Latin grammar into the Chinese language.

This grammatical projection of what he calls 'extended Latin grammar', which is surprisingly close to what Jacques Derrida referred to as globalatinization [*mondialatinisation*], is what has enabled the West to wage its war on spirits [*esprits*] – a war where it assures its control of spirits *through the control of their symbols*, which is to say *by imposing criteria of selection* on their particular retentional apparatuses. Grammatization is the production and discretization of structures (which traverse pre-individual milieux and trans-individual organization, and which are supported by technical or mnemo-technical apparatuses).

There is nothing artificial about these structures: there is no doubt, for example, that very elementary structures of subject and predicate, with verb and object constituting the predicate, exist in language. This is why Aristotle suggests in principle the possibility of uncovering parts of speech forming a logic which nevertheless presupposes the discretization of the Greek idiom. Such structures do not, for all that, exist in every language – not in the same way in any case. The Hopi Indians, for example, do not, according to Benjamin Lee Whorf, denote time.

With this in mind, what can we learn from structural descriptions and what is their significance? What are we to think, knowing that when the Castilian grammarian Nebrija described idioms so as to unify them into a single speech, he affirmed in his dedication to the Queen of Spain that 'language has always accompanied power'?[21] And, above all, what are the consequences of this, in terms of support for control societies, *in the hyper-industrial age which is establishing itself as the third technological revolution of grammatization?*

Grammatization is a war waged on spirits [*esprits*] via the technical development (individuation) of systems of tertiary retentions. It characterizes the process of psychic and collective individuation constitutive of the *unity of the Western world*, and it is spreading increasingly, by way of adoption, into *industrial societies* in general. *Its history is that of a succession of losses of individuation*, as well as of *displacements of the capacity for individuation as a negentropic and idiomatic power.* Today, this history is entering its hyper-industrial stage, which I argue constitutes a limit to the process of Western individuation – and, in this respect, the end of the West. And it is in this sense that Deleuze can say: 'We are no longer Greek, nor even Christian.'[22]

'*Who's* that, *we?*' Nietzsche would no doubt have *repeated.*

31.   A brief history of Western individuation

(b)   Displacements of the capacity for individuation

In the Greek city, with the invention of the alphabet, the preindividual milieu constituting the common fund of the individuals making up the city – itself a process of collective individuation – becomes structurally interpretable. It is in principle, that is, *available to interpretation* (by citizens debating it in the *logos*) by virtue of its *literalization.* This means that *the mnemotechnical mediation of individuation, as the inheritance and interpretation of a pre-individual past, organizes the conditions of individuation.* We will find the same thing at work in our own epoch qua hyperindustrial, but such that it is now the technologies of information and communication that organize individuation.

With the Sophist crisis in the fifth century BC, the interpretability of the pre-individual milieu became a threat to the city-state which was being torn apart by *stasis*, or civil war.[23] It is in this context and on this basis that Plato worked (principally, but not exclusively, in *The Sophist*) towards the *logical reduction of interpretability*, and it is in this way that he established the *axiomatic foundation of the process of grammatization* typical to Western individuation.

The process of grammatization is a *mnemotechnical transformation of the relationship to languages* such that it allows, on the one hand, the *domination of vernacular idioms* and the constitution of realms based on linguistic homogeneity, and on the other, a process of colonization based on the *alienation of the spirits [esprits] of the colonized by the imposition of Western intellectual technology.* The colonized spirits [esprits] being thus 'grammatized'.

The process of grammatization is the basis of political power understood as *the control of the process of psychic and collective individuation. The hyper-industrial age is characterized by the development of a new stage in the process of grammatization*, now extended, in the discretization of gesture, behaviour and movement in general, to all kinds of spheres, going well beyond the linguistic horizon. This is also what constitutes Foucault's *bio-power* – which is simultaneously control of consciousness, bodies and the unconscious.

But, since the unconscious cannot be controlled, the control society is a censorship society of a new kind which is unavoidably incubating an *explosion of drives* – preceded by myriad forms of variously soothing compensatory discourse. Here, where it is not a matter of fearing or hoping, but of 'finding new weapons', that is, of *fighting*, however *cowardly* we may be. Because such is 'the shame of being a man'.

Greece saw the emergence of logic as politics. We are living through the absorption of logic into logistics. This absorption leads to the *reduction* of *projection* – always the setting to work of criteria, and I think projection here starting from primordial narcissism – *to a calculation* for which there is no more indeterminacy, or singularity. I do not at all mean that calculation prevents projection. On the contrary, I have shown in great detail why *all* projection presupposes calculation. Rather, I mean that the takeover of calculation, which has become bioelectronic mechanical technology, *by the sole motivation of capital accumulation*, is *entropic* – where the alphanumeric obsession issuing from Judeo-Greek grammatization generated a negentropy constitutive of the political dynamic of psychic and collective individuation.

Projection assumes a project, and its *reduction* to calculation means that this project is no longer, strictly speaking, an opening to the future – to the extent that this would be essentially indeterminate, and, as such, strictly incalculable – even where calculation can also serve an intensifying role as a generator of singularity.[24] This is why I argued in *Cinematic Time* that this reduction, characteristic of the hyper-industrial age and presupposing the hypersynchronization which is the effective reality of the control society, is also the *imminent possibility of a paradoxical reversal of symbols* (which are always constitutive of synchronization) *into diabols.* An *I* and a *we* that are no longer able to project are effectively condemned to *de-compose*, which is precisely the meaning of *diabelein.*

From the outset, the process of grammatization tends to *control* synchronically individuation. The *we* is always, in one sole movement, but each time singularly (in each epoch constituted by such a *we* which characterizes its psychic and collective individuation – the Greek *we*, for example), simultaneously a configuration of *synchronization* AND of *diachronization*, which is to say, of *differentiation* in the *composition* of its tendencies. And here *criteriology is characterized principally by the way in which it is articulated and arranged with this double tendency of synchronization and diachronization – a tendency that is in principle irreducible.*

At least since the Phoenicians, synchronization has been a grammatization in the sense that it is a *discretization of the content constitutive of the temporal flux of speech.*[25] This is particularly clear with the origin of the Greek *polis* if one considers it in terms of a 'monumental writing machine' – to use Marcel Détienne's expression. This process of grammatization appears as a stage in the evolution of technics and mnemotechnics that has taken place since the beginning of hominization. It is a technical process of individuation which simultaneously supports and undermines psychic and collective individuation.

In *Cinematic Time*[26] I argued that *mnemotechnics*, especially those issuing from the invention of the alphabet, evolve in relative independence from the evolution of *technical systems*. Technical systems go through a succession of epochs of change, while mnemotechnics alter only marginally – until the appearance in the nineteenth century of technologies and industries of information and communication. At this time a fusion of the mnemotechnical system of retentional apparatuses with the technical system of production of industrial goods in general takes place. The consequences of this fusion do not become fully apparent until the twentieth century which it characterizes in every respect. It constitutes a major rupture in that the criteriological control of retentional apparatuses passes over entirely to the side of capitalist investment.

This would perhaps be the determining characteristic of what we might call hyper-industrialization in that it is essentially constituted by the control of all retentional processes. Including the most intimate, including consciousnesses and bodies that are in principle *essentially intimate* – and are thus deprived of their intimacy.

From the end of the nineteenth century we see the emergence of technologies of information and communication productive of a kind of tertiary retention which will radically transform the conditions of grammatization and therefore the process of individuation. After Antiquity the individual as *believer* took over from the citizen, and then, during the nineteenth century, the *worker* took over from the believer. But, as this worker is *progressively dis-individuated by the machine*, the *devaluation of work* becomes unstoppable – from the 'fragmentation of work'[27] to the *stress* of the senior executive, now increasingly demotivated and instrumentalized. It is as though there were a *becoming-machine of the managerial worker*, of the 'senior executive' (which is a kind of reversal of what Simondon says, who still believed that the manager could have a coordinating role). From here on it is clear that *in the hyper-industrial society, the individual is essentially a consumer*.

But, consumption seems to consist in a *tendency towards the annulment of the I/we difference*, such that there *is no longer any individuation*, neither psychic nor collective, but only what I have referred to as the *one*.[28]

32.   Ill-being and acting out: the consumer as individual disfigured by the *one*

The ill-being affecting the present epoch is characterized by the fact that *I can less and less, I can with more and more difficulty, nay, I cannot at all, project* myself into a *we* – neither more nor less than the other *Is* in general.

The *we* is *seriously ill:*[29] the submission of retentional apparatuses,[30] without which there is no psychic and collective individuation,[31] to a criteriology which is totally immanent to the market, to its now hegemonic imperatives, renders the *process of projection* by which a *we* constitutes itself by *individuating itself* practically impossible. The *cultural hegemony* over retentional apparatuses that Gramsci began to theorize in the 1930s, and which is now systematically exercised by capital, *serves as a block in the pursuit of individuation*. The individual ill-being resulting from this state of affairs manifests itself in somatizations, neuroses and obsessional behaviours of compensation or avoidance, or by various rationalizing logorrheas which may be imitative or reactive. In extreme cases it manifests itself in individually or collectively suicidal behaviours, be that of sovereign states, vassals or terrorist groups.

I believe I have demonstrated on a number of occasions, particularly in *Cinematic Time*, that the control of R2 by televisual R3 leads to a process of hyper-synchronization, such that the consumers of the industrial temporal objects that are audiovisual programmes tend asymptomatically to adopt the same secondary retentions, meaning that they make the same selections in their primary retention. This results in a loss of singularity among individuals who, as Deleuze and Guattari say, become 'dividuals'.[32] There is therefore a *dis-individuation* such that the individual's *narcissistic capacity* is first of all excited (including in the hyper-narcissism characteristic of certain spheres of work) before collapsing.[33] Deprived of singularity, they attempt to singularize themselves through products suggested by the market which exploits this misery peculiar to consumption. Narcissizing to excess and in vain, they experience their failure, at which point they finally lose their image: they no longer love themselves and prove to be less and less capable of love. A situation of complete disarray, from which Viagra and pornographic websites are able to prosper.[34]

I will return to the question of porno-graphy with respect to contemporary art and cinema in the final chapter.[35]

This is happening because with modernity, and above all with hyper-industrialization, the temporalities of consciousness are becoming meta-markets.[36] To the definition of modernity, put forward by François Ascher at Cerisy in 2001, as individualization, rationalization and differentiation, I suggested adding 'the systematic organization of the adoption' of industrial products, or the organization of consumption.[37] The hyper-industrial age is determined, therefore, by the fact that economies of scale resulting from the expansion and globalization of markets, especially by way of industrial temporal objects, have become more important than gains in productivity.

The liquidation of narcissism resulting from the submission of consciousnesses to the time of temporal objects affects the *I* just as much as the *we*. And this means that, if the individuation of the *I* is indeed indissociably that of the *we*, and vice versa – where the *I* can only be within a *we*, and the *we* cannot but be constituted by *Is* – then *the blocking of the individuation of the* we *is necessarily also that of the individuation of the* I, *which is to say the pure suffering of this* I. This suffering, when directly manifested, leads to completely uncontrollable acts, which are strictly unpredictable and purely destructive.

If it is true that a consciousness is constitutively diachronic, singular and animated by its own time, then the industrial synchronization described in *Cinematic Time* leads to a *deconsciousization* which is a *loss of individuation*. This can have extreme consequences. I tried to show, for example, that Richard Durn *did not exist*: at least, this is what he wrote in his diary. No narcissism, no self-love, and therefore no respect for anyone else. And yet he experienced the *irrepressible need to exist*, which is to say the need to 'have that feeling', as he wrote. It is this contradiction – the existence of this need, deprived of the possibility of satisfying itself, because the condition of its satisfaction has been destroyed for want of a *capacity of individuation which is also a force of diachronization* – it is this individual drama, as widespread as it is today, that made him a criminal. Durn is a man who ended up acting out. He is one among millions who, suffering from being annulled, from being transformed by the *one* into *Nobody*, are as many Durns in the making.

The synchronization of all consciousnesses is the annulment of the narcissism that I call primordial. When consciousness becomes the object of a systematic industrial exploitation, which is nothing but a process of synchronization, self-love is destroyed. Ill-disposed to itself, consciousness can no longer stand itself: it lives in the untenable. And, not being able to stand itself, not being able to ex-ist, not being able to project itself into a world which has become for it an *unworld*, it can no longer stand others. In the worst manifestations of this crisis, it *destroys* them. This *destruction of others* is a warning sign of the destruction of the *we* as *we* by the *we* becoming a *one*. Others here are representatives of the *we* which it is a matter of destroying inasmuch as this *we*, which no longer individualizes itself, is the thing that is destroying us.

Such is the destiny of the *dividual* of the individual, forsaken when it becomes a pure and simple consumer.

33. From the loss of individuation to becoming-disposable

The *one* therefore designates a loss of individuation, and it is my hypothesis that this constitutes a liquidation of individuation itself: the *one* would be the annulment of a constitutive difference.

AND YET, individuation and *loss* of individuation are *indissociable*. That is, *for individuation to take place, losses of individuation must also take place.* Typically, this is what Leroi-Gourhan says about the emergence of the ethnic group, with the displacements of individuation (of differentiation, in other words) firstly from the flint/cortex distribution towards the ethnic group/technical system distribution – the ethnic group becoming the place of singularity, differentiating itself by reflection and in apparent opposition with technical differentiation,[38] which is also its territorial extension – then from the ethnic group towards the citizen, and then, says Simondon, from the citizen towards the machine (taking place as the loss of individuation characteristic of modernity, which we have already examined). And this is also demonstrated by the history of grammatization, especially where the alphabetic discretization of the temporal flux of speech allows for the emergence of political individuation at the price of a grammatical and idiomatic homogenization of vernaculars.

Today, it has become necessary to study *where* these destructions and fortifications take place. In this respect we clearly need to ask to what extent it is possible to speak of a new form of collective individuation based on *brands* [*marques*] (produced by marketing – and the appellation itself [*marque*] calls for a long commentary): a new form of individuation, organized by companies producing systems of collective individuation as *economic units* substituting themselves for political units. Less on the basis of work than *on the basis of consumption*, which is *more stable* than work – we do not stop consuming – but which nevertheless produce processes of individuation of an extreme fragility (the adoption organized and controlled by marketing) which come to substitute themselves for the psychic and collective individuation of the state.

Such processes of individuation, if it is still possible to speak of individuation here (which I seriously doubt), imply networks – and, as it happens, franchised networks of distribution, for which television networks, carrying publicity announcements as industrial temporal objects, serve very well. We refer here to Naomi Klein's and Jeremy Rifkin's numerous remarks on this subject.[39] The logic of *lifetime value* is that of a loyalty gained through the individualizing attachment of an *I* to a *we* that has been entirely *fabricated by the product or service*, or the range of products and services.

I argue, however, that this individuation might in fact be a disindividuation, leading to what I will call later an *arthropod-tendency*. Because the kinds of individuation produced by marketing do not seem viable and are in all probability very short-lived: they are *disposable*, like everything they produce. Disposability is their logic – this is what was put forward by Hannah Arendt with her concept of durability. And there is a problem of *crossing limits*, which is to say of the *ecology* of the system.

34.   Attention, retentions and protentions in the networks: vampirization

'It is human *attention* rather than physical resources that becomes scarce',[40] writes Jeremy Rifkin, describing what I suggested earlier was a defining trait of the hyper-industrial age. But *attention is not only captured, but strictly produced through the control of retentions and pro-tentions by way of industrial temporal objects.*

This harnessing or controlling of attention could equally be a capture, as in *A Thousand Plateaus*[41] (which is in fact a transduction as Simondon understands it): we will see how this capture leads to a becoming-arthropod (anthill), in an associated milieu modality (according to Simondon's concept) where the consumer becomes the producer of the network *where he* consumes and *which* consumes *him* (which consumes and exhausts his desire).

An *arthropod* surrounded by its prostheses, as though its prosthetic skeleton from now on covered its muscles, like the car where the consumer resembles a ridiculous hermit crab in its shell. And this constitutes a characteristic of the insect, of the arthropod oscillating between the ant (I will come back to this) and the spider on its *web*. But a spider which eats itself: an autophagic or entropic spider. In other words, the consumer, consumed by what he consumes, is *vampirized*, and this development is that of an *(almost) perfect control* leading to the annulment of Eros and Thanatos. Their annulment, that is, as tendencies which – in the tension between them, in the play of effective repetitions – together composed the dynamic of individuation (of difference).[42]

Attention is, through and through, the *holding of retentions* in and by the *object* of attention: *in* and *by* [*dans et par*] in the sense that it is *in* the object that *what is retained* of the object by attention – to the extent that it is attentive – is to be found. While, on the other hand, attention is *attentive* to the extent that it is *anticipatory* [*en attente*], which is to say, in the language of phenomenology, *pro-tended* [*pro-tendue*] and *pro-tained* [*pro-tenue*] by its *protentions* – the object being constituted as an object of attention precisely by *anticipations preceding the object*, anticipating it as the relationship to a future where attention is constituted. Attention which anticipates is in this sense taken *by* the object.

Now, the protentions that draw out [*tendent*] attention and keep [*tiennent*] it attentive, and in a certain sense alert, and which constitute the vigilance of that which anticipates, are themselves *concealed in retentions*: they are what the retentions of the past allow in the projection of the future.[43] It is as an accumulation of experiences in what I have previously called secondary retentions that the horizons of anticipation are formed. These are, in a certain sense, the positive of the negative made up by the retentional residues that fabricate consciousness as the memory of past experiences in the form of secondary retentions. But, as we have seen, the secondary retentions where these protentions are formed filter the primary retentions and pre-cede the possibility of the object of attention.

(These secondary protentions which encounter primary protentions in the object, induced, that is, by the structure of the object itself – just as primary retentions presuppose the structure of the object which may be the interval formed in a melody by two notes – are themselves preceded by what I call archi-protentions. These come from a ground of drives which is in consciousness – but which is unconscious – and which Freud called the death drive and the life drive. This ground of drives is individuated in each consciousness depending on secondary retentions which thus enable the constitution of secondary protentions. Something that Hitchcock understood very well in cinema.)

Attention means, however, projection *in the object* as the constitution of *primary* retention: primary retention is the con-tent of attention – that is, of anticipation – or, if you prefer, its *setting* [*contention*]. But this anticipation that is constitutive of the attention brought upon a given content, an anticipation which is the opening of consciousness *par excellence* inasmuch as it is attentive to its objects, inasmuch as it is 'conscious', is what is 'captured' as attention by way of mnemotechnologies. This anticipation that forms attention is what is literally *flattened* by the hyper-synchronization typical of the hyper-industrial age, where it is transformed into the calculated result of a retentional apparatus, *standardizing* a retentional ground that is in principle *singular* – a ground from which, *precisely because of its singularity*, attentive consciousnesses learn something of themselves through the attention they direct towards the other who is a mirror of their own alterity or their own future possibilities, which is to say of the open incompleteness of their individuation.

It is because the hyper-industrial retention that captures their attention in fact weakens it, finally exhausting it, that consciousnesses 'zap': the system *destroys* attention as it captures it, and tends to engender inattention, the opposite of what it wants. It is a kind of absolute *dis-traction*, a distraction *without attraction*. Disindividuated by retentional standardization, mediatized consciousness tends no longer to project protentions which are therefore increasingly lacking. Chaos [*débandade*].

This is also why the hyper-industrial retentional apparatus attempts to create new kinds of attention capture as it takes advantage of the hyper-segmentation of markets (or consciousnesses) enabled by digital media – by way of the 'personalization' of the means of ensnarement.

The attention of consciousnesses is captured and produced by way of *networks*, these constituting the most advanced stage of the mechanical technical system – inasmuch as it is becoming a mnemotechnological system, and in its industrial integration of the production of material goods with the production of symbols. But *the development of networks is a stage in what needs to be analysed as a technical individuation.* More precisely, *the technical individual is no longer only the machine, but the technical system inasmuch as it is networked.*[44] From this point on, psychic individuation and collective individuation are inscribed in and submitted to the concretization of the network, in the sense in which Simondon described mechanical individuation as a *process of concretization – and which I argue follows the process of grammatization discussed above.*

35. The standardization of modes of access to the pre-individual milieu and the particularization of singularities

The 'users' or 'targets' of the network become functional elements of that network.[45] Through the example of a tidal power plant Simondon demonstrates that water, as *an element of the natural geographic environment*, becomes a *functional* element – and in this capacity a *technic* – of the Guimbal turbine, the sea becoming an associated environment that he refers to as techno-geographic. In a similar way, through the establishment of methods for the analysis and synthesis of their behaviour, information and communication technologies functionalize their users for innovation and auto-adaptation to behavioural developments. But here, the equivalent of the orchid – as a device for capturing the energy of the Charlus bumblebee[46] (or the wasp) – is that which exhausts the energy of this bumblebee-equivalent (or wasp) through the synchronization of retentions which, in their differentiation from the retentions of other bumblebees, stimulate its potential libidinal movement (woven out of the motifs that constitute the singularity of its fantasies). There is thus a *functional integration of the consumer* (user, target, etc.) and of his 'consciousness' in the associated environment formed by the new techno-geographic-human reality (it is no longer simply a question of physical geography). And this means that *the historical and symbolic milieux are also functionalized* such that *the user becomes a function of the system he is using*, his individuation being subjected to that of the network – 'two beings which have absolutely nothing to do with each other' says Chauvin, cited by Deleuze and Guattari. Which is not, however, strictly true, and here is the question that remains to be thought through.

As for this subjection of the user-consumer to the *process of concretization* constituted by the network, we will see that it corresponds pretty well to the system of capture constitutive of an anthill, and that it poses a real question concerning *libidinal ecology* – perhaps glimpsed by Lyotard in his *Libidinal Economy*.[47]

Such are the systems of *user profiling*, of tele-action and interactivity that exploit and functionalize return pathways, *just in time* and the development of geo-localization, *where the one who consults a database is himself a part of that database*, etc. I argued elsewhere that it is a question of the establishment of *new forms of calendarity and cardinality*.[48] These forms of cardinality of control are evoked by Deleuze in the following terms:

> We don't have to stray into science fiction to find a control mechanism that can fix the position of any element at any given moment – an animal in a game reserve, a man in a business (electronic tagging). Felix Guattari has imagined a town where anyone can

leave their flat, their street, their neighbourhood, using their (dividual) electronic card that opens this or that barrier; but the card
may be rejected on a particular day, or between certain times of
the day; it doesn't depend on the barrier but on the computer that
is making sure everyone is in a permissible place, and effecting a
universal modulation.[49]

In this logic, *disjunctions* are possible. Recent technological developments allow us to imagine a transformation of the technical
system permitting the invention of new processes of individuation
and the reinvestment of singularities – the models of functional
integration of usage and user knowledge developed by the free
software community, for example. *At the same time* as technological developments allow us to envisage perspectives of rupture with
the mass-model, however, they also lead to an unprecedented
aggravation of the loss of individuation.

Individualization as personalization, *one-to-one*, hyper-segmentation of markets, etc. is the transformation of *singularization* into
particularization by digital grammatization, which, measured by
the effectiveness of its control, is infinitely more powerful: it *per-
formatively* produces models, which self-engender (by way of
self-organization) and which it projects into the network, as with
the orchid and the image of a wasp. These are then adopted very
'naturally', the process of psychic, collective and technical individuation being itself a process of adoption. The digital discretization of all movements in individuation effectively allows for their
ordering, treatment, calculation and imitation in the production
of *categorial attractors*.

*But, the particularization of the singular is the standardization
of modes of access to the pre-individual milieu*, which precedes
and conditions psychic and collective individuation in that they
are the two sides of one same process – *by way of* grammatization,
which is the third prong of individuation. This implies equally a
tendency towards the liquidation of what Simondon calls the
trans-individual, understood as the co-individuation of the *I* and
the *we* in the tension (and attention) of their endless difference.
In this respect, the analyses put forward by research into cognitive
(or 'immaterial') capitalism as a new process of subjectification
seem to me to be at the same time attractive and unconvincing:

there where we find the convocation of singular resources, and, along with this, the invitation made to the worker to 'self-production' in the workplace, we also find the systematic exploitation of the general frustration of the bodies and minds of workers by the management techniques of 'human resources'. This leads to *hyper-narcissistic compensation behaviours* and a well-known hyperactive *pathology*, which in reality only serve to prepare or foreshadow the psychic and familial collapse resulting from the corrosive effects of stress on the individual. In this respect, the legitimization of the apparatus of capture seems particularly naive when Muriel Combes and Bernard Aspe write that:

> . . . it is not individuals who interiorize the 'business culture'; it is rather business which from now on will look 'outside', that is at the level of everyone's day-to-day life, for the competencies and capacities it needs.[50]

Because, in the first place, it is hyper-industrialization as the industrialization of daily life that formats 'everyone's' day-to-day life as functionally in service of the business world (particularly *via* prostheses, such as the mobile phone, that are used indifferently at work and in the private sphere) – in service, that is, of the company, which in the control society has replaced the factory. Symbolic misery affects these executives and other 'resources' just as much as it does the suburban working-class ghettos.

36. The hyper-modern stage of grammatization as a generalization of calculation

As the site of individuation of a *we*, the human pre-individual milieu constitutes a trans-individuality. As opposed to animal individuation, human individuation (understood as an incomplete movement) is total and permanent, and its meta-stability is not based on the relative stability of the species that supports the pre-individual ground of the animal – something that Aristotle sensed in the *Peri Psyches*.[51] Psychocollective trans-individuation is supported by the tertiary retentions originarily constitutive of technical objects (inasmuch as they are epiphylogenetic). Something not articulated as such by Simondon, even though this is practically what he wrote, almost without realizing it.[52]

This means that individuation is not double but *triple*; *psychic, collective and technical*, each one unthinkable without the others – they are in a *three-pronged* transductive relationship.[53] In the process of technical individuation there appeared, in the Neolithic period, a mnemotechnical sub-system which separated itself from the *technical system* responsible for technical individuation more generally. It is within this sub-system that the process of grammatization develops. With the arrival of the industrial and mechanical era the process of concretization described in *On the Mode of Existence of Technical Objects* is established. But the development of mechanical concretization leads towards the becoming-network of the technical system, so the mnemotechnical becomes mnemotechnology, and is thus, along with the user-consumer, functionally assimilated into the technical system. And the totality of this development is determined by the process of grammatization.[54]

The current loss of individuation is a stage of grammatization where the *three individuations (psychic, collective and techno-mechanical) generalize formalization through calculation*, with the performative effects that this involves: effects of (non-)meaning affecting consciousnesses at the deepest level – in their most *intimate affects*, as unconscious retentional/protentional aggregates. That is, grafted onto the ground of drives constitutive of the deepest pre-individual reality of trans-individuation.

From ancient Greece until the twentieth century, grammatization consisted of describing idioms, and, through their description, altering them so as to control them. The hyper-industrial stage of grammatization, however, necessarily leads – with text becoming hypertext, for example, such that it is accessible via the intermediary of 'search engines' – in the direction of the *formalization of the reader himself, of this reader inasmuch as he constitutes an idiolectic grammar.*

Leroi-Gourhan, who was the first to speak of hypertext, has demonstrated that with the development of libraries in the sixteenth century, assistance with orientation and thus with reading – in the form of filing cards, catalogues and indexes, etc. – became indispensable.[55] According to him, this meant an exteriorization of the nervous system, and by extension an exteriorization of imagination: from the tables of contents and authority lists to the 'magnetotech'[56] that is today's networked global digital system – passing by way of the Jacquard loom and the emergence of data processing with Hollerith's machine in 1887 – at stake is the same process of externalization of the functions of reading and computation.

But, in the hyper-industrial age, this exteriorization no longer allows for a correlative interiorization – taking place as a dia-chronization as it interiorizes a synchronic structure, which it singularizes by idiomatizing (as idiolect). This is because it entails the liquidation of narcissism as the condition of eroticism which is itself the condition of all interiorization: the criteriology imple-mented by the process of exteriorization itself is transformed because its hegemonic imperative has become the optimization of the process of adoption, from now on conceived in terms of con-sumption. *Theological, epistemological and political criteria, which always projected trans-individual forms of singularity, are abandoned.*[57]

(It is as though, along with God, the *polis* and the *episteme* had also de-ceased, which is to say, science as pure knowledge. Pure here meaning free from any relation to development and industrial techno-logy, if not from *techne* – originally understood *as knowl-edge, or, in other words, as art*. And it is perhaps here that the question of the relation between 'aesthetics' and 'politics' is *most fully* posed: perhaps we are living through the end of politics, as the culmination of a typically Western process of psychic, collec-tive and techno-logical individuation. And this is taking place when, and *because*, the aesthetic sphere is being absorbed into the economic sphere of production – what I have called elsewhere the absorption of the *he* [*il*]. But it is precisely here that aesthetics and politics must perhaps, through the formation of *another* relation, invent *new names*: with the question of aesthetics being from now on *global*, we are awaiting another thinking of the *kosmos* as the *future* of all cosmopolitics understood as the *invention of the world*.)

It is necessary to speak of the *formalization of the reader* to the extent that reading behaviour is *categorized* when it is exteriorized and formalized by the tools of computer-aided navigation. These categorizations may be very basic (*user profiling*, for example) or more sophisticated (as is the case with what I have conceptualized as 'societies of authors' ['*sociétés d'auteurs*'][58]), when knowledge shared by readers is categorized (that is, when trans-individuated secondary retentions are formalized, and thus 'tertiarized'). It is my hypothesis that these categorizations are only just beginning and will go much further (leading, for example, to 'societies of authors', as *societies of readers endowed with the means of themselves formalizing and inscribing their singular readings* in the information that has been read, so that these formalizations can be pooled, constituting a tool to help with the navigation of that information). But, on the other hand, and for the moment, these tendencies are embodied by search engines which do not formalize and intensify singularities, but rather reduce them by, for example, accentuating mimetic behaviour and generalizing a ratings logic in what claim to be personalized access procedures – as with Google.

37. Digital pheromones

Grammatization generally modifies what it formalizes, whether that be in a synchronizing or a diachronizing sense. So, Greek grammatization brought about the emergence of the figure of the citizen – meaning it intensified its diachronic power as a political individual – while at the same time allowing for the liquidation of vernaculars, ultimately leading to the exteriorization of symbolic functions. In the hyper-industrial epoch, this exteriorization seems to lead to entropy, or to the total liquidation of the diachronic by hyper-segmentation, taking place as the particularization of the singular.

A reader, or, more generally, a speaker (but this is true for every signifying structure) is the bearer of their own idiolectal grammar, which constitutes their singularity and which resonates with grammars that are more idiomatic and which may be closer or further from it. Idiolectality is the situation of every local idiom in its relation with the more generic idiom that surrounds it. This relation of the specific to the generic, or the diachronic to the synchronic, is precisely what allows for the formalization of Simondon's concept of individuation as the co-individuation of an

I and a *we*. But, at the current stage of mechanical exteriorization, loss of individuation takes place as a tendency to confuse the *I* and the *we* in the *one*: resulting in an *idiomatic exhaustion*, together with a loss of narcissism and the blocking of individuation. There are no longer individuals, but sheep-like, tribalized, particulars, moving towards a social organization of arthropomorphic, reactive, cognitive agents, which tend no longer to produce symbols, but, like ants, *digital pheromones*.

Because an idiolect – or the grammar that prevails in an individual, constituting them in their singularity in its relation with a surrounding grammar – can in principle be formalized, like any other idiom. I say *like* – this can happen *within the limits* I expounded previously in 'The Discrete Image',[59] which is to say that a discretizing and descriptive formalization such as this is, in reality, more than a description: it is an inscription or a modification. It is 'knowledge' of individuation which is not knowledge since it is its performative transformation, as I recalled by way of warning. But this can happen in the process of individuation of another, who can in this way be brought under control, manipulated and alienated: this is what happens in what Sylvain Auroux describes as Western grammatization in the context of colonization.

The pursuit of individuation as an attempt to understand it – what I am doing right here – always has a political stake: it is an *intervention* in its *conditions*. I am appealing for a '(non)-knowledge' (that is, an arsenal along with its mode of implementation) that would intensify diachronicity, or the power of singularization. While at the same time I argue that hyperindustrial knowledge of this individuation – now become global *via* the formalization of readers/navigators, produced as consumers on the internet – is a development that tends to annul the future, or the very temporality of its readers. That is, their desire.

As constitutive of the mnesically preserved experience of the individual, secondary retentions constitute an access to the pre-individual ground of an individual, which is itself organized idiolectically, or according to regularities giving it coherence. Primary retentions effectively represent selections within paradigms which are idiolectical organizations of secondary retentions, as well as syntagmatic organizations mobilizing rules of concretizing composition which are also secondary retentions (previously 'performed' formulations). In other words, one must analyse retentional organization on both Saussurean axes (which clearly do not exhaust all dimensions of meaning production).[60] The singularity of secondary retentions, as an *original grammatical organization* (semantic or syntactic), is what forms idiolectical contention/retention – it is the *con-tent* of the idiolect in a broad sense: this can be extended way beyond linguistic protention and retention. Every discretization proceeds by way of these categorizations. But the digitalization characteristic of the hyper-industrial age of mnemotechnologies formalizes all of these grammes, the body included.[61]

38. From cognitive to reactive

The *one* seems here to put itself forward as the *becoming-arthropod of society* (human society becoming if not a society of insects then at least a multi-agent system – whether these are cognitive or reactive agents, they are in any case prosthetized). The allegory of social insects allows us to recall the critical stakes of the modes of regulation resulting from the technological and industrial transformation of pre-individual milieux in the hyper-industrial context – as well as, correlatively, from the generalized exteriorization of symbolic, mental and motor functions into the prostheses that increasingly surround the living body.

Hyper-synchronization tends to eliminate the diachrony of the *we*, which is, equally, the consciousness of the *I*. It does this by submitting the cardino-calendaric apparatus, for which it forms the meta-retentional system,[62] to the criteria of the economic sphere – by integrating and submitting, therefore, mnemotechnics to the global technical system of the production of consumer goods.

This cardino-calendaric integration represents a passage to the limit – as it is understood in dynamic systems theory – which means that *the conditions of viability of the system are put into question*. It leads to a situation anticipated by Leroi-Gourhan as follows:

> At the techno-economic level the nature of human integration is no different from that of animals having territories and shelters. It is quite otherwise at the aesthetic level, integration being based on

purely symbolic references accepted by society under a rhythmic convention that puts days and distances within an artificial network. The separation between free time and space, on the one hand, and domestic time and space on the other, remained reasonably wide until quite recently, except in urban environments where a completely humanised framework was always a token of the efficiency of the city's apparatus. The infiltration of urban time has taken place within a few decades, initially affecting only long intervals of time through the regularly periodic character of transport facilities but now spreading to all moments of the day to suit the rhythm of radio and television broadcasts. A superhumanised space and time would correspond to the ideally synchronous functioning of all individuals, each specialised in his or her own function and space. Human society would, through spatiotemporal symbolism, recover the organisation of the most perfect animal societies, those in which the individual exists only as a cell.[63]

'The infiltration of urban time' designates submission to the time of work, transportation, shopping, etc., up to and including media time as the time of the hyper-masses. 'Superhumanization', as the setting up of a completely synchronous society, would be the liquidation of the social – if one bears in mind that Leroi-Gourhan (and Simondon in different terms) described the social in this sense as a tension between the individual and tradition,[64] where the individual inscribes their idiomatic singularity, or their diachronicity.

Leroi-Gourhan formulated this hypothesis of a *pure final synchronization* in 1965. At the time, 46.5 per cent of French families owned a television set. Today, this figure has more than doubled – almost the entire population. At the beginning of the twenty-first century, the synchronization of consciousnesses is heading towards perfection, to be capped off by future mobile communication and hyper-media devices. These will follow their users everywhere they go, as mobile phones do today, will be able to tell them where they are at all times and will solicit them depending on their geographic location, adapting themselves at the same time to the characteristics of their super-urbanized environment as they pass through.

The synchronic system anticipated by Leroi-Gourhan can now be almost perfectly realized: with the advantage that it allows for *individual specialization*, as in an anthill – for *the organic division of work*, in the same way that with social insects like ants we find soldiers, foragers and nurses, etc.

In other words, super-humanized society would lead to what 'multi-agent' systems theory calls a community of reactive agents. In *Disorientation* I gave a brief introduction to this, inspired by the work of Dominique Fresneau[65] and Jean-Paul Lachaud:

> An anthill consists of separate classes of 'individuals' identified by their behaviours for 'task-completion': reproduction, care of larvae, foraging for food, an 'inactive' class. The number and proportion of individuals in each class is stable. If a 'sociotomy' occurs[66] – if part of a class of individual ants is removed – the anthill's equilibrium will be re-established as 'hunters' become 'caretakers', and so on. The hypothesis is that environment reinforces or inhibits the various specialisations of individual 'agents' through the fact that each ant emits chemical messages, called pheromones, confirming the anthill's informatics modelling through a multi-agent system. These trace emissions are most salient here, in that the informatics model sees these agents as 'reactive', meaning that they have no memory of 'their own' behaviours. There are effectively two models of multi-agent systems: one in which the agents are called 'cognitive', having an explicit awareness [*répresentation*] of their behaviours and their past behavioural experiences, and the other consisting of 'reactive' agents, without self-awareness or memory, responding to a stimulus/response schema. The behaviours of the individual agent in the anthill clearly follow the latter model. But if agents have no memory of previous behaviours; if their specialised behaviours are determined by other agent's behaviours, there must be a model of collective behaviour inscribed somewhere, at least temporarily. In the case of ants, pheromones are the chemical traces inscribed on the ants' habitat as support – the anthill and the surrounding pathways marked by individual hunters – and as a mapping of the collective.[67]

In fact, *individual connections* do not stop multiplying. An individual connected to global networks, who is already geo-localized without knowing it on a web of variable links, emits and receives messages to and from the network of servers, where the memory of collective behaviour is recorded – just like an ant which, secreting its pheromones, inscribes its behaviour on the territory of the anthill, decoding and commanding, by way of a gradient, the behaviour of other ants. And, to the extent that the integrated cardino-calendaric system brings people to live increasingly in real-time and in the present, to dis-individuate themselves as they lose their memories – that of the *I* just as much as that of the *we* to which it belongs – everything happens as though the 'cognitive' agents that we still are tend to become 'reactive' agents, which is to say, *purely adaptive*. No longer inventive, singular and capable of exceptional behaviour which in this sense would be unexpected or 'unlikely' – radically diachronic in other words – in short: *active*.

Deprived of this possibility of diachronizing itself in unforeseeable ways, of in some way regularly *excepting* itself and inventing against the necessity of adaptation, the *I*, suffering from being remote-controlled, may suddenly take on *destructively* unpredictable and exceptional behaviour. This *becoming-reactive* – which may also be understood in Nietzsche's sense as resentment – incubates the explosions that we find in Leroi-Gourhan's hypothesis, to which the current cardino-calendaric integration seems to be drawing closer. The 'human' individual only exists here as a cell which is, precisely, a 'reactive agent': he is *dis-individuated*. Which is as much as to say that he is literally *de-brained* [*décervelé*]. Exteriorized, become superfluous and fallen into obsolescence, his central nervous system is from now on useless, even harmful: the individual 'cell' should be perfectly subjugated to the 'supra-individual organism'.

> Because of the development of its body and brain, through the exteriorisation of tools and of the memory, the human species seemed to have escaped the fate of the polyparium or the ant. But freedom of the individual may only be a stage; the domestication of time and space may entail the total subjugation of every particle of the supra-individual organism.[68]

The exteriorization of human memory, which has allowed for the accumulation and transmission of individual experiences, would end up in the creation of a reactive network, as though this experience were from now on entirely standardized and disembodied.[69] With this hypothesis, the man-technic coupling would only have needed individual liberty – over a few thousand years – in order for the system to develop correctly and form a 'supra-individual organism' which, at the moment of its total planetization, ultimately resembles that of the *perfectly synchronous* organizations of what we call social insects.

And yet, Freud objects:

> [T]he bees, the ants, the termites – strove for thousands of years before they arrived at the State institutions, the distribution of functions and the restrictions on the individual, for which we admire them to-day. It is characteristic of our present condition that we feel we should not be happy in any of these animal states or the roles assigned in them to individuals.[70]

39.   Overwhelming majority, tiny minority

The reader will perhaps object in turn that such a hypothesis is nothing but a pure fiction, and that it does not correspond in any way to the reality of their daily lived experience. To this I would respond, firstly by reminding the reader that this fiction describes an asymptotic tendency with which it is necessary to compose,[71] and secondly, by asking him not to forget that, since he still has the will and ability to read a work like *Symbolic Misery*, he is without doubt a representative of a social category that is currently very limited in size, and on the path to extinction, it would seem, unless something extraordinary happens.

It will also be objected, and not without reason, that there is still invention, and plenty of it, even in the midst of the processes I am describing. And I agree. I say that we must analyse these inventive practices: I have done so elsewhere, I have not stopped doing so since at least 1978. And I would add that I believe that I am led nearly all the time, in all my actions, by a concern to develop these kinds of practices. I would like to underline, however, that this fight for invention is taking place on the terrain of a game between two tendencies that are going head-to-head, and that everything is in place for the one to put down the other. At the moment, it is practically a war, the result of which seems to me to be completely uncertain. And it is clear that there is no evidence that a kind of invisible hand or New Providence will be there to assure that the necessary counter-tendency will be automatically preserved, preserving the tendency itself at the same time.[72]

The vast majority of the urban population of large industrial countries live in conditions that are increasingly less bearable. They carry out professional tasks that are evermore thankless, stripped of all meaning for those who carry them out – as far removed from any meaning as it is possible to be – tasks with generally extremely trivial purposes, paying the working population enough to enable the adoption of increasingly standardized consumer behaviours. The things consumed bring so little life to the consumer that an *increasingly abyssal* feeling of frustration results, which itself results in an *always more frenetic intensification of this consumption*. This frustration increases, therefore, along a *slope* that is exponentially orientated towards a straightforward drop, where the only question is *knowing when it will stop*. We are a long way from 'self-production' . . .

As for the inhabitants of the planet who do not live in industrial countries – in the overwhelming majority of cases, they are reduced to a state of unspeakable misery, the colossal, immeasurable scale of which is in all likelihood without precedent in the history of humanity.

It became common at the end of the twentieth century to speak of humanity as though those making up this *we* were all, more or less, in an equal condition. This so-called equality points to an absolute fiction, and the growth of inequality in living conditions is such that the groups making up different communities and social groups often have very little in common. Despite the levelling illusion of this reality produced on a daily basis by the world's media, these groups sometimes become practically incompatible – while *we*, *you*, who are listening to this conference or reading this book, *I*, who am delivering it or writing it, we who have access to human works that Kant said were the fruits of the spirit, we are becoming a tiny minority.

40. 'Us' and 'them'

We, who make up this tiny minority, we live in privileged, if not very privileged urban milieux: in districts that still look like towns, where we sometimes visit restaurants worthy of the name, where our children go to schools in which it is still just about possible to learn something, even if this is becoming increasingly difficult, where we can visit theatres and cinemas showing a variety of films, where we can wander in streets with shopkeepers selling quality goods. But we know NOTHING, for the most part, of the conditions in which our fellow citizens live, which have often become detestable, if not unbearable.

While most of the people living in our industrialized countries are still able to feed themselves, dress themselves and find somewhere to live (even if an ever increasing and evermore IMPOSING number, right next to us, sometimes outside the building where we live, do not really have access to these perks of civilization), the vast majority of these people are seeing their living conditions degrade to the point where they themselves are physically and morally degraded – stuffed with bad food, dazed, to a point that it is hard to imagine, by always more demeaning culture industries. Not being yourself affected by this development which nevertheless covers ever more groups, you stand prudently to one side, at the risk of blinding yourself and of becoming capable of *denying without reserve* [*vergogne*] existence itself.

Without *reserve* [*vergogne*], that is, without the *shame* [*honte*] that is 'one of the most powerful incentives towards philosophy'. Another risk is that you fail to realize that you as well have perhaps *already begun* to allow yourself to be absorbed by this process of generalized degradation, becoming slowly but surely less and less capable of seeing what, like a *new era of non-knowledge*, here takes shape as the *limping energy of chance* – that, for example, of Thelonious Monk – so long as weapons, concepts, pianos, tuned, attuned, repaired and prepared, and other instruments are found.[73]

IV

Tiresias and the War of Time
On a Film by Bertrand Bonello

I know that it's a sin, roses aren't God's invention but man's, who took what God had created: he transformed it. But I thank God for putting me on earth today and not at a time when roses did not exist.

Bertrand Bonello

Then, realising that no one could see me, I decided not to let myself be disturbed again for fear of missing, should the miracle be fated to occur, the arrival, almost beyond the possibility of hope (across so many obstacles of distance, of adverse risks, of dangers), of the insect sent from so far away as an ambassador to the virgin who had been waiting for so long. I knew that this expectancy was no more passive than in the male flower, whose stamens had spontaneously curved so that the insect might more easily receive their offering; similarly the female flower that stood here would coquettishly arch her 'styles' if the insect came, and, to be more effectively penetrated by him, would imperceptibly advance, like a hypocritical but trusted damsel to meet him half-way. The laws of the vegetable kingdom are themselves governed by increasingly higher laws. If the visit of an insect, that is to say the transportation of the seed from another flower, is generally necessary for the fertilisation of a flower, that is because self-fertilisation, the insemination of a flower by itself, would lead, like a succession of intermarriages in the same family, to degeneracy and sterility, whereas the crossing effected by insects gives to the subsequent generations of the same species a vigour unknown to their forebears. This invigoration may,

however, prove excessive, and the species develop out of all proportion; then, as an antitoxin protects us against disease, as the thyroid
gland regulates our adiposity, as defeat comes to punish pride, as
fatigue follows indulgence, and as sleep in turn brings rest from
fatigue, so an exceptional act of self-fertilisation comes at the
crucial moment to apply its turn of the screw, its pull on the curb,
brings back within the norm the flower that has exaggeratedly
overstepped it.

Marcel Proust

41. Cinematography

Throughout the twentieth century, large-scale industry seized on
image technologies, making the image into a major weapon in its
transformation of the world into a market where absolutely everything is now for sale – starting with the spectators' time of
consciousness. And a veritable war is raging across all kinds of
media for access to these temporal consciousnesses. The compe-
tition among the media makes this butchery of consciousness –
this becoming-pig which Gilles Châtelet spoke of[1] – into a vile
spectacle.

But it is not simply a case of gaining access to the temporalities
of consciousness: it is a matter of transforming them and, as far
as possible, synchronizing them so as to control and desexualize
their bodies, with *nuptial life in general* having become superfluous. Because it is a question of slowly but surely reducing their
diachronic singularities: their libidinal energy. A diabolical paradox
because it is precisely this energy that is sought as pollen to be
made into honey. The search for that which is *thus* sought tending
not only to make it unfindable, but *nonexistent*.

This war is not only amongst the media: it is a war against
aesthetic experience in general, which is to say against art and
thought (other than mathematics, all thought is aesthetic, and
always, at the origin of a concept you will find an affect: this is
what I tried to show in *Passer à l'acte* – in other words, for me it
has never been a matter of simply ratifying Deleuze or of repeating
Spinoza like a parrot, authors I had in any case not read when
swarms of affects produced their first concepts in me).[2]

The necessity of a *functional reduction of singularities* has led
to the submission of almost every human experience to aesthetic

and affective – as well as cognitive and informational – *control*. Electronic technologies have enabled the establishment of 'control societies' as well as the implementation of the concept of *lifetime value*, which was invented by marketing so that the systematic and industrial exploitation of individual experience could be realized to the highest degree, transforming this experience into a fully controlled conditioning.

This has led to a situation of symbolic misery where *aesthetic* conditioning in its essence constitutes an obstacle to aesthetic *experience*, whether or not that be artistic. It is in this way that tourism, now that it has become industrial, ruins the viewpoint of the traveller who has become the consumer of a washed-out time.

But the main technological advance allowing for this state of affairs – for this submission of aesthetics to industrial development, which represents a total revolution in the human way of life in relation to what happened during the thousands of years separating it from Lascaux – is cinematography, defined here as a technology allowing for the mechanical restitution of movement. From this point of view I argue, as in *Cinematic Time*, that television is, from a technical perspective, a simple electronic development of cinematic technology.

Cinema is also, however, an art. I would like to show why this art has a very particular responsibility in the context of control societies: it is *par excellence* the aesthetic experience able to fight aesthetic conditioning on its own terrain. But this also means that the present situation with respect to man's self-image, with respect, that is, to his narcissism, must be evaluated – in the sense in which Freud spoke in *Civilisation and its Discontents* of the change in the way humanity has thought of itself since the death of God.

42. The nightmare of blinding images

The industrial exploitation of image technologies in the service of an unbridled expansion of markets by the conditioning of all experience has led, as *image technology*, to the destruction of the primordial narcissism of individuals – the destruction of that which enables individuals to *project* the unity of an *I* in a fashion clearly as fictional as it is indispensable. A projection through which they are able to enter into social relations with other *I*s to form a *we* which, as a collective narcissism, represents the liveable space of an aesthetic experience that can be nothing other than a sharing, the 'sharing of the sensible' of which Jacques Rancière sought to speak. It is this *we* that Freud called *culture* (*Kulture*) – actually translated as *civilization*.

But, by destroying primordial narcissism, the unbridled industrial exploitation of image technology (of cinema, of which television is a sub-category) has eradicated the very possibility of *seeing* images.[3] Producing blinding images, the industrial exploitation of images is their straightforward destruction – since there is no image that is not seen.

Not being seen, the image can become either an oracle of the blind seer (as Tiresias), or a 'reality' where the *symbolic* is neutralized – a nightmare reality. There is no doubt that we are living in an epoch of nightmare aesthetic,[4] from which oracles occasionally emerge. An example of this image-nightmare-reality to my blinded eyes: Arnold Schwarzenegger becoming governor of California.

North America, country of cinematographic images (televisual included), has essentially established itself as a world power through the mastery of cinematographic technology, industry and art – and now of digital technologies as well, which will soon allow for the complete control of access.[5] Political power understood very quickly the incomparable power of cinema: as early as 1912 an American senator said that 'trade follows films', and Jean-Michel Frodon has summarized the American understanding of cinematographic power by arguing that films and television programmes garnering the esteem and money of populations were worth more than GIs.[6] Isn't this how the West won the Cold War?

43. The return to war, properly speaking

To what extent, however, has the esteem of Western images been earned in this way? Because it seems, since 11th September at least, that GIs are having to replace films – even while 11th September was a unique global television event. That *unheimlich*, not quite live broadcast, which was doubtless the most watched in History – more so than the live lunar landing of Neil Armstrong.

Will the return of the televisual repressed put GIs before cinema in the long term? Whatever the reply, the question assumes that cinema, like GIs, is a weapon. It is a political weapon (making the unity to the States of North America), an economic weapon (domestic and global trade follows films) and a militaro-diplomatic weapon (where cinema, television and the armed forces together form a system). If GIs' weapons are once again *before* cinema, however, this is because the unbridled exploitation of cinematographic power – particularly of this power inasmuch as it has also become televisual – has led ultimately to the liquidation of the narcissism of the viewer, of his *power of projection*, to the point where he *can no longer see images* – whether he is a humiliated viewer from the 'Southern countries' or someone from the industrial countries of what we call the North, lobotomized, or rather, blinded like the transsexual or *trans-instinctual* [*transpulsionnel*] body that is Tiresias with her punctured eyes.

44. The spectatorial equipment of projection and cinema's cathartic function

Tiresia is a film of exceptional, almost unbearable, power by Bertrand Bonello (2003): a *film of the blind* [*film d'aveugle*], and an aid brought to the blind that we are, *as* it is brought to the roses that are pruned in the film.[7]

In *Introduction to a True History of Cinema*, Jean-Luc Godard argued that the projector, in the cinema, is the viewer himself:

> When the viewer looks, the camera is inverted, he has a kind of camera in his head: a projector which projects. And for that matter, when Lumière invented cinema [. . .], when he invented the camera, at the same time it was used as a projector, it was the same machine for the two things.[8]

An image only arrives at the viewer to the extent that he projects it, which is to say, expects it.[9] And yet, if he is to be affected, the image that he expects must surprise him, which means it must be, for him, unexpected. The only solution to this apparent contradiction is that the viewer *bears in himself* what is unexpected for his consciousness – and cinema is what enables him to *project this expected unexpected*, which is to say to *liberate* it. There is a cathartic function to cinema which is overburdened by the industrial exploitation of images, even if, and all the difficulty is here, it is always possible to look at any image from a projective perspective. And this without taking into account the fact that from its beginnings cinema is industrial, and, in this respect, 'commercial', tele-visual even – I will come back to this. In other words, there is *no* way for this projector viewer to distinguish an image that is *in itself* projective from an image that is *in itself* destructive[10]: the image is literally pro-duced by the viewer. The fact remains that certain images *tend* towards the destruction of spectatorial narcissism.

This also means that cinema, inasmuch as it is always industrial, *is* the unlikely future of industrial society.

A projective horizon of expectation is constituted by the narcissistic structure of expectation, or desire. But the narcissism referred to here – which is the structure of the *psyche* as such in that it implies a mirror – implies reflective surfaces that have a history: media which are more or less deforming and informing, forming a whole morphogenesis of viewing and of the affect more generally – from shaped flint to technologies that integrate *everywhere* image artefacts, making the still or moving image into an ordinary content of individual tele-communication, and so generalizing tele-vision to an extreme degree – and tele-control [*télé-commande*] and tele-surveillance [*télé-surveillance*] along with it.

But this generalized tele-visual system is what annihilates every horizon of expectation, which means every unexpected. So at a time when moving images are everywhere, there is no longer any image: there is no longer any kind of viewing capable of finding itself affected, in a sense where the affect would be the discovery of the singularity of that which is thus affected.

It is against this that the last filmmakers are struggling.

And it is in this way that, to the misfortune of the Iraqis, GIs, as bodies and souls armed *to kill*, have moved in front of images as temporal industrial and cinemato-graphic objects made *to capture* [*seduire*] their bodies and souls – their consumer bodies which, in the global economic war, it is a case of submitting to expectations fabricated in their entirety by marketing.

It is now a matter of understanding how such a fabrication is possible.

45. Protentions and drives: On incarnation

A film, we now know, is a temporal object in the Husserlian sense: this is what Kuleshov's experiment with the image of Mosjoukine shows. Mosjoukine's face 'expresses' different moods – in the viewer's consciousness – depending on the different shots that precede it, while it is always the same shot of Mosjoukine's face. In Husserl's terminology, this means that the shot of Mosjoukine's face is seen from the perspective of the 'primary retention' (that is originary) of the preceding shot. In the same way, in music, a note only sounds as a note because it *retains* in it the *relation* which binds it to the preceding note, which is what we call an interval, or, in Pythagoras' language, a *logos*.

A temporal object – a melody just as much as a film – is an aggregate of primary retentions combined by the consciousness that looks at or listens to the temporal object in various ways – where protentions, or expectations, are produced.

In the same film, however, everyone does not see the same thing, and this is because primary retention is a primary *selection*. Consciousness does not retain everything. This is why, if I watch a film again, I do not see the same thing the second time, even though I am aware that I am watching the same film. The object is the same, but the phenomena it produces are different. This does not happen because the film has changed, but because *I* have changed. We knew all this already. But what we must now add is that it is my *expectations* that have changed because my memory has changed. It might be, for example, that I have *already* seen this film.

Memory is made up of secondary retentions, and these filter the primary retentions, or the primary selections, taking place as I watch a film: secondary retentions, *as the horizon of expectations* of my consciousness are the criteria of selection. What I do not expect, I do not see. But it happens that *I expect the unexpected*: how can this be explained?

If each of us sees a different film in front of the same screen, this is because we project what these secondary retentions allow us to filter in the material presented to us by the film, which is thus transformed into protentions which are the *reflected* images of *our* most unexpected expectations – which is to say, the least conscious, the most deeply buried in the *unconscious* which is woven of secondary retentions, and is like their *body*.

Because our memories are different, traversed by singular secondary retentions which only belong to us, we see different things in the same film. But because these memories are *incarnated*, our secondary retentions form, with and in our bodies, the energy of the drives that extend our desires – on the ground of these most elementary of proto-expectations, that are the *drives*.

46. Protentional capture by collective secondary retentions (CR2)

Television tends to annihilate the diversity of individual secondary retentions, so that the singularity of points of view [*regards*] on images collapses. It is television's vocation to synchronize individual temporalities of consciousness so as to constitute global markets: consciousnesses belonging to bodies, the behaviours of which it is a matter of controlling with a view to *accentuating their massively consumerist expectations*.

Marketing very quickly seized on television because it understood that audiovisual technology would allow for individual protentions to be controlled, to be aroused and channelled, while exploiting the archi-protentions that are the drives – the materials of the desire that motivates every point of view [*regard*].

Beyond primary and secondary retentions, there are tertiary retentions: objective memorizations, memory-objects, technics of recording and memorization, etc. Some of them allowing for the production of industrial temporal objects: this is the case with the phonograph and the cinema. Through the control of audiovisual tertiary retentions, it is possible to intervene in the way in which consciousnesses function, in that they never stop arranging primary retentions through the intermediary of the filters of their secondary retentions – particularly through the mobilization of secondary retentions shared by viewers, so forming the secondary retentions of a *we* and not only of an *I*. This is how the trans-individual in Simondon's sense is constituted: through the production of *collective secondary retentions* (CR2), generally supported by tertiary retentions, R3, which may just as well be works as technical objects, things, fetishes, etc. – *goods* being a limit case of this *fetish character of all things.*

And words are such CR2 productions: this is how trans-individual significations are established. Of course, everything depends on knowing why a particular CR2 has been adopted, or selected and therefore retained, and by whom, when another has been erased into inexistence. This is one of Nietzsche's *organological* (mnemo-technical) questions in the second essay of *The Genealogy of Morality*. Because in the *grey* of genealogy,[11] on the ground from which the colours of images lift off, there is a *retentional arsenal which serves the fabrication* of CR2.

The power over spirits, the retentional control of drives and the enslavement of desires through the reduction of idioms (of singularities, of 'idiocies', by the instrumental *stupidity* [*bêtise instrumentale*] which is also their *particular condition, every* idiom itself being always already a 'stupid instrument' [*instrument bête*], a blinkered dialect), through the reduction of idioms, therefore, submitted to grammatization, etc., this is all, always the fruit of the technologies of production of CR2, or the R3 set to work by grammatization, of which cinema is an epoch.

The fabrication of CR2 is what happens, for example, in *Gone with the Wind*: it is from the collective memory of the War of Secession that we find the establishment of the retentional/protentional work through which Scarlett appears projected by her American viewer – from the North or the South, but as their common perspective. It is also from the memory of *Gone with the Wind* that I watch *A Streetcar Named Desire*, projecting onto Blanche, played by Vivien Leigh, the forever vanished effaced face of Scarlett.[12] Or again, it is because I remember *La Dolce Vita* that I am narcissistically overwhelmed by the scene in *Interview* where Anita Ekberg sees herself thirty years on in the Trevi fountain with Marcello Mastroianni: here, my secondary retentions as viewer of these two films by Fellini are shared not only with the theatre, but with those of Anita Ekberg, Marcello Mastroianni, Federico Fellini, and even the fictional Japanese journalists who are present in the scene (like clones of the *paparazzi* in *La Dolce Vita*).

The extraordinary power of cinema.

47.   Cinematographic art as *anelpiston*: 'There is no place for hope' because there is the unhoped-for

A filmmaker (but this is true of every artist) produces tertiary retentions, (temporal) memory objects, which are materially and therefore *spatially* projected, as ephemeral as they may be. Across these, he enables a *we*, or a sensible community, to experience the singularity (as much collective as individual) of its protentions – of its *most unexpected* expectations, inasmuch as they express the strength of its desire. This is how a *we* invents itself, and becomes what it is. The artist plays with the secondary retentions of his audience *via* the organization of primary retentions, which he arranges in the form of an apparatus of tertiary retentions. This is what Kuleshov demonstrated.

In this way, the artist seeks to produce aesthetic experiences that are always singular – to the extent that they allow for the projection of the *unexpected* that supports *every* expectation (this is what Heraclitus called the unhoped-for, *anelpiston*), and which, in its essence, grants an always renovating *new*, however deeply buried in the archaic it may be, in *the most ancient*: in the 'domain of the drives' [*le 'pulsionnel'*].

It is because they mobilize the ground of the drives that temporal audiovisual objects have an unprecedented symbolic efficacy. But the audiovisual culture industry tends to substitute itself for the artist in the production of tertiary retentional arrangements, in order to produce homogeneous collective secondary retentions which lead to the straightforward elimination of the singularity of individual points of view [*regards individuels*], and of the bodily behaviours of the consciousnesses to which these points of view belong: it is thus a case of standardizing the behaviours of consumption. This is possible because tele-vision is a network broadcasting temporal objects at fixed times, allowing for the mass sharing of secondary retentions, which results in the accentuation of increasingly homogeneous criteria for selection from primary retentions. To the point that, no longer able to project itself, individual singularity here disappears, and ultimately it is primordial narcissism, or the condition of desire, that collapses.

Such is the result of this transformation by which the aesthetic experience of the projection of a meaning [*sens*] (a point of view [*regard*], for example) is turned around into the aesthetic conditioning of this same meaning, from now on enslaved to the consummation of 'images' that can no longer be seen.

The material of the drives that 'protends' every awaiting is between life and death, between Eros and Thanatos. All cinematographic stories are one way or another a play between Eros and Thanatos – including the most stripped-down of films, as is the case in the sumptuously interminable first scene of Antonioni's *Eclipse*. This ground of drives is very often summoned 'below the belt' as well: it is not summoned in order to *produce a difference* in the repetition constitutive of every expression of a drive, but, on the contrary, to reinforce the narrow identity of the repetition through the homogenization of retention criteria.

48. Up against temporal default, the most unexpected expected

Art in general is that which seeks to temporalize differently, so that the time of consciousness of the *I*, supported by the unconscious ground of its incarnated memory, is always diachronic. It liberates through its affirmation the narcissistic unexpected of consciousness's singularity, which can be projected in a *we* through the intermediary of the *screen that every work of art represents*.

This is an experience. But television, on the contrary, seeks to synchronize consciousnesses, to neutralize them as consciousnesses, confining them in the most impoverished modality of the repetition compulsion. Such is the *control through affects* in control societies: we are talking about the most powerful aesthetic control possible, much more so than Guattari's electronic collar, since it is truly a voluntary servitude. Inasmuch as it eliminates the diachronicity of singular desire, or its unexpected, this kind of control inevitably leads to the liquidation of narcissism, or of the unconscious and of desire as a socialization of the drives. In other words, television inevitably leads to the explosion of the drives, or to acting out. September 11 is thus the date of a terrifying battle in the war of time unleashed by the attempt to synchronize diachronies which are uncontrollable precisely because they are singular.

We find here behaviour of suicidal tendency for industry: the market cannot develop without desire.

Time has always been the object of the battle constitutive of aesthetic experience – as the battle against temporal default, *right up against* it [*tout contre lui*]. How to make oneself available to the work of art inasmuch as it represents an apparatus calling for an availability without limit to the unlimited, most expected unexpected of the work? This is the question that is constitutive of all aesthetic experience of time.

This is the *sensible*: it is not position, but dis-position. But, we are now living in a war where the articulation of primary, secondary and tertiary retentions has become the permanent and daily production of an industrial control *via* what are called flux industries [*industries dites de flux*]. And this control is naturally and essentially an obstacle to the disposition and availability necessary for aesthetic *experience*. What this control aims to eliminate is precisely *availability to time* inasmuch as it is in essence *uncontrollable singularity*.

49.   Tiresias and the revolutionary arsenal

In this respect, *Tiresia*, and for that matter *Le Pornographer*, are exemplary films: the question of these films is that of cinema's relation to desire, the responsibility of cinema in relation to desire or in relation to the sexual.

Bertrand Bonello's is a cinema of sexuality such that it integrates the question of *technicity* – the technicity of cinematographic images just as much as the technicity that allows for the *transsexual body*, which is to say, in a certain way, the angelic body, or its opposite, since the transsexual is the *body of two sexes*.

This cinema recounts the violence done to a transsexual by a priest who punctures her eyes, and the mutation of the victim into a blind seer – and is like a graft of Sophocles' Tiresias onto the lame Oedipus who will become the very figure of Freudian desire.[13] This film is therefore like a rose, like one that is 'absent from all bouquets' of all kinds of hybrids. And that is not all, this film demonstrates that we must *dechristianize and tragedize* these questions of desire and technics: we must revisit Tiresias and the question of vision as pre-vision pre-monitory of the blind, which is to say as protention beginning from the tragic condition of he who, like Epimetheus, gropes in his essence – the tragic condition that is, in other words, the condition of technics in ancient Greece (at least, I tried to demonstrate this in *The Fault of Epimetheus*).

'Without *reason*', the rose is nevertheless tragic, and Bonello's cinema poses the tragic question of cinema, which is to say of tele-vision that has become pre-vision: he poses it as being tragically porno-graphic. The question of the pornographic film is the question of cinema such that the possibility of the porno-graphic is at the heart of *all* cinema, and so it is never a case of simply *opposing* cinema and television, but of criticizing television *through cinema*, which is always already inhabited by television as *power*: of *experiencing this composition that gives roses without reason*, for which one can only *thank* God. *Even* if he is dead.

Afterword

For Caroline

After having dedicated *Love, Love Yourself, Love One Another: From 11ᵗʰ September to 21ˢᵗ April* to the people who voted for the National Front, I went so far as to insist, during a radio show,[1] that we should address ourselves to National Front voters *with friendship*.

I know to what extent this might be problematic or shocking, and that it also begs the question: 'Who is this *we*?' This is not, however, a provocation or posturing, but the basis of my thought, and even constitutive of my thought of the *we*.

What I am here calling *symbolic misery* is first of all that suffered by the voters of this extreme right-wing party – a party with which it is clearly out of the question for me to speak – and to which they bear witness, as horrific as their *testimony* might seem.

Refusing to speak to the National Front does not in any way mean refusing to speak to its voters. I would even say that *addressing oneself principally to them*, before anyone else is, in my eyes [*à mes yeux*], the *absolute priority*, *however unbearable the reality to which they bear witness* might be – bear witness, that is, with their *vote*, as the *only possibility for symbolic exchange that they have left, before the worst*. Even if this address is for the most part very indirect, and even if for me it is mainly *concerned* with these witnesses and that to which they bear witness precisely *where they CANNOT PROPERLY hear me* [*m'entendre*].

'In my eyes' [*à mes yeux*], and I repeat the expression: 'in my eyes', by which I mean just as much my eyes as *philosopher* as my eyes as *citizen* and *man capable of shame*, of being ashamed, capable, in other words, of reserve, of *aidós*.[2]

50. Eris and stasis

It is absolutely appalling – and almost *shameful* – that those who claim to think and act politically *do not see* that *there are only two possibilities*:

- either we agree to speak *with* or *towards* [*vers*] or *for* the National Front's voters, addressing them even as a *priority*, to the extent that they are the most direct witnesses to the suffering that is ruining public life – and whatever their own take on this matter, this remains a *testimony*, however wretched [*misérable*] it may be, to deny it would be shameful: it would be to deny them humanity;
- or we deny them the status of *citizen*, and in this case we would not be protected for long from civil war, because these are indeed the stakes.

Civil war obsessed the Greeks, who experienced it many times, and they called it *stasis*.

For my part, I, like Aristotle, consider *philia* to be the *condition* of public life (which, for a long time, was named the city, *polis* – a name that I keep, for want of a better alternative, even if I believe, and as I have already weighed up in a previous chapter, that since the process of Western psychic and collective individuation is now complete, this name is without doubt obsolete. I will explain this in *La Technique et le Temps 4. Symbols et diaboles, ou la guerre des esprits* [*Technics and Time 4: Symbols and Diaboles, or the War of Spirits*]). The *condition* of public life is *philia*, which is to say, a familiarity and a *friendliness* [*amicalité*], as it is so well translated by Jean Lauxerois. Friendliness without which *no dialogue* is possible.

But, *dia-logue* is the condition of the public space: of its *dia-chrony*, beyond any *totalizing syn-chrony* of a *one* no longer having anything of a *we*. And no longer believing in dia-logue would be a terrible indication of political and spiritual, as much as symbolic and philosophical, misery. Not to imagine its possibility would, for that matter, be to have *already put a stop* to dia-logue; and we call this chattering. Dia-logue is concerned. Including in the soli-loquy that is the 'internal dialogue' that Gadamer spoke of.[3] This is what I have elsewhere called the *fragility* of freedom.[4] But a philosophy or a politics that *did not believe* in dia-logue would be nothing but the philosophy of vanity and the vanity of philosophy, the politics of vanity and the vanity of politics.

Étienne Tassin is certainly perfectly correct to reiterate, with Arendt and against Habermas, that politics is not exhausted by language. But the dia-logue I am speaking of here is not simply language: it is *symbolic exchange*, including that supported by *all labour activity*. It is in this way that Marx defined the proletarian: in that he is deprived of the possibility of individuating himself through work, as Simondon would say, he cannot *signi-fy*. And, since the proletarian has no 'spare time' apart from work, he is purely and simply deprived of any symbolic existence, which is to say, of *any existence full stop* – if not in struggle, which is what the Communist parties understood both so well and so badly.

It is aesthetico-symbolic existence in the public space that is the city [*cité*] as *agora* that bestows the *rights of citizenship* [*droit de cité*] on the citizen. And this existence is not possible except in the sphere of a *philia* shared between Hestia, goddess of the hearth or private space, and Hermes, god of exchange and circulation in the communal public space that Étienne Tassin attempts to rethink.

If *political dia-logue* is a space of *peace*, however, it is not a space that is consensual and free from conflict, quite the contrary: Hesiod sings in praise of *eris* as the girl emulation of Heraclites' *polemos* (combat), from which the best emerges – the *ariston* that Arendt also speaks of.[5] But Hesiod also laments the reverse of this *eris*, and as adversity, since Eris, 'daughter of Night', is also – like *eris* meaning discord in modern Greek – she who stirs up conflict between those who nevertheless belong-among-one-another [*s'entre-appartiennent*] in *philia*.

This struggle is not in any way a war, and this is why it is not *stasis*: it is the conflict between brothers *that can be decided by justice*, thus for Hesiod and for Perses – even if justice can prove to be unjust – and it is also the conflict between citizens or between parties. And this is also why *stasis* is not the destiny towards which all *eris*, or discord, in the city leads. And it is why Tassin is wrong to translate *stasis* by 'discord': it is a matter of going beyond this Platonic conception of conflict in the *polis*. *Stasis* certainly means discord, but there are several kinds of discord, of which one, *eris*, is the most characteristic game of the *agora* and of the *agon* in which it consists – *stasis* must therefore be translated as *civil war*. This is what Marx sought to think, but failed, unable to see the symbolic, aesthetic and erotico-libidinal (relating to the drives [*pulsionnelle*]) dimension of the question. He was perhaps unable to see, therefore, the political sense, beyond political economy, of that which he called the *class struggle*, even if he glimpsed it in his first period through his critique of Hegel.[6]

The *polis* is essentially discord *of the many* making up the *one* promised by political *becoming*. This discord, which is the very *dynamism* of Western political psychic and collective individuation, is precisely what Plato wanted to annul. And it is precisely what is targeted by the asymptotic tendency leading to what I have here illustrated by way of the allegory of the anthill.

Platonism as metaphysics has imposed itself and realized itself, it has become *Wirklichkeit,* or effective reality. The 'anthill' is an allegory of the de-composition of the dia-chronic and the synchronic, which cannot establish themselves except in their *composition*, except in the tense, *transductive,* relationship where the *tensors of singularities,* constituting the 'libidinal economy' as discussed in *Civilisation and its Discontents,* are formed. It is by denying the hypomnesic, which is to say, the techno-logical dimension of all symbolic exchange, that Platonism manages to impose the reduction of *techne* to pure calculation – the aim of this metaphysics being to *control all affect* and to *deny any right to interpretation,* which is to say, the free and indeterminate singularity of souls inhabiting bodies. Which is why, for this Platonism realized today in cultural capitalism, poets and artists are the enemy (which can, however, always be bought: money can do *almost* everything, if not *absolutely* everything), while the workers can be nothing but slaves excluded from symbolization according to the singular mode of their diachrony, which is what Simondon referred to as their loss of individuation.

But, this symbolic misery, which is now spreading beyond the proletariat – since it affects the consumers *that all of us are*, since it affects our children, our friends, our parents, since it contaminates our most intimate environments, like the air that poisons all the inhabitants of certain places on the planet, whether they are rich or poor, propertied or proletarian – makes the environment uninhabitable. This symbolic misery is *all the more unbearable* because it is symbolic, and not only 'physical' – as though symbols were condemned to turn into diabols.

This is why the future is so threatening.

And it is also why I repeat, and I will never stop repeating: in the conflict that sets me against those who vote for the National Front, I offer them my *friendship*.

Notes

Foreword

1 Stéphane Mallarmé, *Divagations*, translated by Barbara Johnson (Cambridge, MA: Harvard University Press, 2009).

2 Published in English as *To Love, To Love Me, To Love Us* along with *How I Became a Philosopher* in the two-volume edition *Acting Out* (Stanford, CA: Stanford University Press, 2009).

3 As Gilles Deleuze wrote in *Negotiations*, translated by Martin Joughin (New York: Columbia University Press, 1990), p. 223 [translation modified]. I give a more detailed commentary on this passage below.

4 G. Deleuze, *Negotiations*, p. 233.

I Of Symbolic Misery, the Control of Affects, and the Shame that Follows

1 This section develops thoughts presented in an article published in *Le Monde* on 10 October 2003 and subsequently broadcast by France Culture on the afternoon of 11 October 2003.

2 Culture, and aesthetic experience more generally, of which art is one dimension, cannot be reduced to the alibis of cultural 'exception' or 'diversity', however valid and necessary international agreements and technical measures on rights might be. It is through these alibis that *aesthetic experience* is made into a sub-category in global affairs.

3 See below, p. 10.

4   Jacques Rancière, *Dissensus: On Politics and Aesthetics*, edited and
    translated by Steven Corcoran (London: Continuum, 2010); *The
    Politics of Aesthetics: The Distribution of the Sensible*, translated
    by Gabriel Rockhill (London: Continuum, 2006).

5   'Confinements are *moulds*, different mouldings, while controls are
    a *modulation*' (G. Deleuze, *Negotiations*, p. 178).

6   The French here reads: 'son *devenir porteur d'avenir*'. I have
    attempted to maintain a notion of becoming *and* carrying, and to
    this end have used the verb 'to bear', with its two meanings of
    bearing a course and bearing something within [trans.].

7   Particularly in *Aimer, s'aimer, nous aimer. Du 11 septembre au 21
    avril* (Paris: Galilée, 2003).

8   'Commodity fetishism' can only exist because *economic exchange
    is ultimately libidinal*. The 'denunciation' of this fetishism by
    Marxism is, therefore, an illusion: it is part of the essence of a com-
    modity to be a fetish. And no object would appear in the world
    without the simultaneous projection of the *fantasy* by which it
    appears. But the critique of the *harnessing* of libido by commodity
    fetishism in its destructive mastery of libido is by no means an illu-
    sion: it is even the most urgent political demand.
        This note is in response to a talk given by Jean-Luc Nancy at
    Ircam on 17 December 2003, with an eye to preparing a discussion
    to take place during the symposium I am organizing from 26 May
    to 2 June 2004, with Georges Collins at Cerisy, entitled 'L'organisation
    du sensible' ['The Organisation of the Sensible'].

9   Jean Lauxerois, 'A titre amical', postface to *L'Amicalité* (translation
    of Books 8 and 9 of Aristotle's Nicomachean Ethics (*A propos*,
    2002), p. 85.

10 *De la misère symbolique 2. La catastrophe du sensible* (Paris:
    Galilée, 2004) [*Symbolic Misery 2: The Catastrophe of the
    Sensible*].

11 In a similar vein, it is both interesting and strange to look at the
    government website: www.jesuismanipule.com

12 See Bernard Stiegler, 'Le temps des attrape-nigauds. Manifeste pour
    une écologie de l'esprit' ['The Time of Scams: Manifesto for an
    Ecology of Spirit'], *Art Press*, special issue '*Internet all over*', Nov.
    1999 and *Technics and Time 3: Cinematic Time and the Question
    of Malaise*, translated by Stephen Barker (Stanford, CA: Stanford
    University Press, 2011).

13 On the loss of participation, see this work, and also *Aimer, s'aimer,
    nous aimer*, p. 43. On the loss of the individuation of the worker,

see *Technics and Time 1: The Fault of Epimetheus*, translated by Richard Beardsworth and George Collins (Stanford, CA: Stanford University Press, 1998), ch. 1.

14 G. Deleuze, *Negotiations*, p. 178.

15 Plato, *Protagoras*, 322a–322e.

16 B. Stiegler, *Technics and Time 1: The Fault of Epimetheus*.

17 B. Stiegler, *Technics and Time 2: Disorientation*, translated by Steven Barker (Stanford, CA: Stanford University Press, 2009).

18 ' "How do you give a memory to the animal, man? How do you impress something on this partly dull, partly idiotic, inattentive mind, this personification of forgetfulness, so that it will stick?" [. . .] perhaps there is nothing more terrible and strange in man's prehistory than his *technique of mnemonics*.' Friedrich Nietzsche, *On the Genealogy of Morality*, translated by Carol Diethe (Cambridge: Cambridge University Press, 1994), second essay, para. 3.

19 B. Stiegler, *Technics and Time 3: Cinematic Time and the Question of Malaise*.

20 Heraclitus, fragment 23: 'They would not know the name of justice, if it did not exist [the unjust]'.

21 Normally 'vergogne' would be translated as 'shame', but since Stiegler is marking a difference between 'vergogne' and 'honte' (which also is normally translated as 'shame'), I have introduced a similar distinction in the English text. In order to do this, I have turned to etymology: 'vergogne' comes from the Latin 'verecundia' the meaning of which is close to bashfulness, so I have translated it as 'reserve' (this also fits well with the character traits of the Goddess Aidos) [trans.].

22 To maintain this distinction, 'malaise' will be translated by 'malaise' and 'mal-être' by 'ill-being', throughout [trans.].

23 *Susceptibility* is the condition for the plasticity of mortals always in becoming; see, for example, Plato's *Charmides*. But it is also the origin of resentment.

24 But we must find a weapon in this lack of *philia*. 'The word friendliness [*amicalité*] here names the unthought that Greek *philia* would have kept in reserve, or the secret of a relation to self and a relation to the world that would reside in the word's lack of meaning: "somewhere in the fracture" says Katos Axelos.' J. Lauxerois, *L'Amicalité*, p. 86.

25 Gilles Deleuze, *Negotiations*, pp. 172–3 (my emphasis).

26 *Negotiations*, p. 181.

II   As Though We Were Lacking

1   This chapter is based on the text of a paper given, at the invitation of Sarkis, during the exhibition *Le monde est illisible, mon coeur si* in Lyon on 2 May 2002. The exhibition was organized by Thierry Raspail at the Museum of Contemporary Art in Lyon and ran from 2 February to 27 May 2002. A first version of the chapter was published in the exhibition catalogue.

2   Bernard Stiegler, 'Le temps des attrape-nigauds. Manifeste pour une écologie de l'esprit' and *Technics and Time 3: Cinematic Time and the Question of Malaise.*

3   This is not true of readers. Contrary to what Wolfgang Iser thinks, a text is not a temporal object: the time of its unfurling is determined by the reader; this is not the case with a listener.

4   On this point, see *Aimer, s'aimer, nous aimer*, Part 1; *Technics and Time 3: Cinematic Time and the Question of Malaise*, ch. 1; *Technics and Time 2: Disorientation*, ch. 4.

5   Even if, inversely, practising music and joining in at musical events was more widespread than it is today.

6   I have developed this point of view on several occasions, particularly in a discussion with Rodolphe Burger in the *Revue de literature générale*, no. 2, POL, 1996 (based on his article 'Loop', *Review de literature générale*, no. 1, 1995), and in *Inharmoniques*, no. 1, Ircam/Bourgois, 1986. Peter Szendy published a fine book from this same perspective, *Ecoute* (Paris: Minuit, 2000), after having organized a colloquium on the subject, published as *L'Ecoute* (Paris: L'Harmattan, 2000).

7   See Joëlle Farchy, *La Fin de l'exception culturelle?* [*The End of the Cultural Exception?*] (Paris: CNRS Editions, 1999). It is because I believe that analogue reproduction affects the way music is made and not just how it is listened to that, ten years before this paper was given at the Musical Research Group, I was able to argue at l'Ircam that the music of Charlie Parker (inventor of bebop and modern jazz), in its coordination of phonograph and saxophone, is another extremely important musical phenomenon.

8   The analyses of *Interview* that I had developed in *Technics and Time 2: Disorientation*, and then in *Technics and Time 3: Cinematic Time and the Question of Malaise.*

9   The 'Koulechov effect', which shows that it is editing that conditions the effect of a shot, is a particular instance of what Husserl calls 'primary retentions' in his analysis of the temporal object. On

this point, see the chapter entitled 'Tiresias and the War of Time' below.

10 Especially chapter 3: '*I* and *We*, The American Policy of Adoption'.
11 On the question of the family in the twentieth century, see François Truffaut, *Farenheit 451*, and Bernard Stiegler, *Aimer, s'aimer, nous aimer*, p. 33.
12 The concept is developed in the first three volumes of *Technics and Time*, and also in this work, p. 34.
13 I come back to the mysterious and primordial question of the unexpected in Chapter IV, 'Tiresias and the War of Time'.
14 There is no reference in Stiegler's text for this or the following quotation from Descartes. I have therefore provided my own translations [trans.].
15 Even if we don't all know *every one* of the songs.
16 I return to these issues at length in the forthcoming *La Technique et le Temps 4. Symboles et diaboles, ou la guerre des esprits*.
17 See Bernard Stiegler, *Technics and Time 2: Disorientation*, ch. 1, 'The Orthographic Epoch'.
18 Alain Resnais, *L'Avant-Scène Cinéma*, no. 263, March 1981, p. 7.
19 The French title of this film was at the centre of a court case that was won by Alain Resnais. The arguments used are of particular interest here. See *La Gazette du Palais*, 29 and 30 April 1998: 'Mr. André Halimi upholds that the film, *Same Old Song* [*On connaît la chanson*], which is currently showing in theatres and distributed by Arena Films, reproduces exactly the title of his book published in 1959 and his radio shows broadcast in 1974–5. He upholds that this represents an obvious breach of copyright of his works, or at the very least an unfair usage of the aforementioned, which represents, for him, a clearly unlawful interference [*un trouble manifestement illicit*] according to the meaning of the specified text.
'These words – "on connaît la chanson" – represent, according to the dictionary *Robert de la langue française*, a figurative and familiar locution.
'The use of this common expression is based in everyday language, and so the rights claimed by M. André Halimi on the basis of paragraph 1 of article L112-4 C. propr. intellect., are not clear for the urgent applications judge [*juge des référés*] but require an appraisal by the trial judge [*juge au fond*].
'Moreover, whatever memories the works of Mr André Halimi might have left in the consciousness of popular music lovers, the risk of confusion between these – in the case of the book, an investigation into the "artistic, economic and social aspects of the pop

song", and in the case of the television and radio shows, interviews with celebrities talking about their impressions of the songs of the era – and Mr. Resnais' film – which is a comedy based on the behaviour of six characters on the "theme of appearances" with brief extracts of songs inserted into the dialogue – is not sufficiently clear to provide sufficient evidence for the claimed unlawful interference.'

20   'I am against women – right up against them' [*Je suis contre les femmes – tout contre*].

21   See www.ecrannoir.fr/critiques/chanson-htm.

22   Cited by Vance Packard, *The Hidden Persuaders* (New York: Pocket Books, 1957).

23   See above, p. 15.

24   V. Packard, *The Hidden Persuaders*.

25   Cited by Jeremy Rifkin in *The Age of Access* (London: Penguin, 2000), p. 145.

26   'I have two loves, my country and Paris . . .'.

27   In *Technics and Time 1: The Fault of Epimetheus*.

28   'J'm'en fous pas mal/Il peut m'arriver n'import' quoi/J'm'en fous pas mal/J'ai mon amant qui est à moi/C'est peut-être banal/Mais ce que les gens pensent de nous/Ça m'est égal/J'm'en fous.' A more literal translation which sacrifices the rhyme scheme might read: 'I couldn't care less/Anything can happen to me/I couldn't care less/I have my love who is mine/Maybe it's banal/But whatever people think of us/It's all the same to me/I don't care' [trans.].

29   The last version of the couplet is different in Edith Piaf's song, and of particular interest for an understanding of Camille's character, in a way by inversion. At the end of the song, the lover *having left*, the returning couplet becomes: 'J'm'en fous pas mal/Il peut m'arriver n'import' quoi/J'm'en fous pas mal/*C'est* mon *passé* qui est à moi [It's my *past*, which belongs to me]/C'est peut-être banal/Mais ce que les gens pensent de *vous* [But whatever people think of *you*]/ Ça m'est égal/J'm'en fous.'

30   Quelque chose est devenu moche/Et c'est cassé/J'veux pas que tu t'en ailles.

31   Tu sais bien/Ce n'est rien/Le temps passe/Et ça revient.

32   Ça s'en va et ça revient/C'est fait de tout petits riens/Ça se chante et ça se danse/Ça revient et ça retient/Comme une chanson populaire . . .

33   Tu préfère mourir que de te rendre.

34   C'était la dernière séance/C'était la dernière séquence/Et le rideau sur l'écran/Est tombé.

35 Ça, c'est vraiment toi!/Ça se sent/Ça, c'est vraiment toi !/Ça se sent, que c'est toi!/Ça se sent, que c'est toi!

36 Je vais, je vais et je viens/Entre tes reins/Je vais et je viens/Entre tes reins/Et je/me re/tiens . . .

37 Je t'aime/Oui je t'aime . . .

38 See below, 'Tiresias and the War of Time'.

39 See *Aimer, s'aimer, nous aimer*, p. 43.

III Allegory of the Anthill

1 This chapter is based on a paper presented at the 'Ecole supérieure de commerce' in Paris on 15 September 2003, during a conference entitled 'L'individu hypermoderne' organized by Nicole Aubert and François Ascher.

2 On this subject I have written: 'To describe postmodernity as being outside modernity would be to overvalue the definition of modernity in a periodization of the history of philosophy and to undervalue the immense effect of the Industrial Revolution as rupture. The chasm between Rousseau and Marx is an infinitely greater one than that between Nietzsche and us, though this does not mean that "postmodernity" is an empty concept: *The Postmodern Condition* is a very important book. However, it is vital precisely to situate its interest in and sense of this deceptive age of modernity' (*Technics and Time 3: Cinematic Time and the question of Malaise*, ch. 4, para. 3a, p. 242).

3 Jean-François Lyotard, *The Postmodern Condition*, translated by Geoff Bennington and Brian Massumi (Manchester: Manchester University Press, 1984), p. xxiii.

4 'I think that Félix Guattari and I have remained Marxist, in our two different ways, perhaps, but both of us' (*Negotiations*, p. 171).

5 'It's definitely Foucault, along with Heidegger but in a quite different way, who's most profoundly transformed the image of thought' (*Negotiations*, p. 95).

6 Gilbert Simondon, *Du mode d'existence des objets techniques* [*On the Mode of Existence of Technical Objects*] (Paris: Aubier, 1958).

7 Which clearly means that he was in the past: I in fact argue for an originary technicity in human individuation, and I will come back to this below. It is, however, necessary to note that Simondon is not completely clear on this point – even if he is sure of his definition of the worker as equipped body. This incertitude regarding the status of technics in Simondon weighed heavily on the philosophy

of Deleuze. On this point, see Bernard Stiegler, *Technics and Time I: The Fault of Epimetheus*; 'La maïeutique technologique de l'objet industriel' ['The Technological Maieutics of the Industrial Object'] in *Autour de Gilbert Simondon* (Paris: Albin Michel, 1994); 'Technique et individuation dans l'œuvre de Simondon' ['Technics and Individuation in Simondon'], *Futur antérieur*, Spring 1994; and Jean-Hugues Barthélémy, *Sens et connaissance à partir et en deçà de Simondon* [*Meaning and Knowledge from and before Simondon*], doctoral thesis at the University of Paris VII, supervised by Dominique Lecourt.

8   Sylvain Auroux, *La Révolution technologique de la grammatisation* [*The Technological Revolution of Grammatisation*] (Brussels: Mardaga, 1993).

9   'Marx, for example, has superb analyses of the problem of discipline in the army and workshops. The analysis I'm about to make of discipline in the army is not in Marx, but no matter: What happened in the army from the end of the 16th and the beginning of the 17th century practically right up to the end of the 18th century? An enormous transformation in an army that had hitherto been essentially constituted of small units of relatively interchangeable individuals, organized around one commander. These small units were replaced by a great pyramidal unit, with a whole series of intermediate commanding officers, of non-commissioned officers and technicians too, essentially because a technical discovery had been made: the gun with comparatively rapid and calibrated fire' (Michel Foucault, 'The Mesh of Power', translated by Christopher Chitty in *Viewpoint Magazine* (http://viewpointmag.com/the-mesh-of-power/).

10 This last point will be further developed in *La Technique et le Temps 4. Symboles et diaboles, ou la guerre des esprits* (forthcoming).

11 See above, p. 17.

12 Which can be retained as *relations*: primary retentions are effectively relations. In a melody, for example, these are the notes in arpeggio that form intervals and chords, and in a sentence they are the syntactical and semantic links. It is in this connection that Olivier Lartillot suggested during the seminar that I chair at Ircam that the paradigmatic and syntagmatic games (according to the Saussurean understanding of these terms) that define an idiolect should be defined as secondary retentions organizing the selection and the setting in relation of primary verbal retentions.

13 This theory is elaborated in *Technics and Time 1: The Fault of Epimetheus*, and picked up again in *Aimer, s'aimer, nous aimer*, p. 63.

14 See *Technics and Time 2: Disorientation* and *3: Cinematic Time and the Question of Malaise.*

15 See *Technics and Time 3: Cinematic Time and the Question of Malaise.*

16 See *La technique et le Temps 4. Symboles et diaboles, ou la guerre des esprits* (forthcoming).

17 On this point, see *Aimer, s'aimer, nous aimer*, pp. 74–6.

18 I say 'in principle', meaning that this double articulation of individuation (of which the doubling of the *I* by the *we*, and vice versa, is one aspect) is based on this principle, but that this principle is fragile. My thesis is precisely that the hyper-industrial age tends to transgress this principle, which is a disastrous and untenable state of affairs. And in this respect the war of spirits has taken a new direction; completely new and as yet unthought.

19 We should not confuse what we are here calling techno-logical with the mnemotechnological age, which follows from the mnemotechnical age of alphabetic writing and the printing press.

20 McLuhan says that in this sense cinematography is the recording of life itself. See Marshall McLuhan, *Understanding Media: The Extensions of Man* (New York: McGraw-Hill, 1964).

21 See Sylvain Auroux, *La Révolution technologique de la grammatisation*, p. 93.

22 Gilles Deleuze, *Two Regimes of Madness*, translated by Ames Hodges and Mike Taormina (Los Angeles, CA: Semiotext(e), 2007).

23 In this respect, I do not share Etienne Tassin's opinion on the question of conflict in the city-state as elaborated in his excellent recent book *Un monde commun. Pour une cosmopolitique des conflits* [*A Common World: For a Cosmopolitics of Conflicts*] (Paris: Le Seuil, 2003). The conflict of the city-state, when it is not bellicose but rather constitutive of politics (which is the *peaceful system of conflict*), is not *stasis*, but *eris*. On this point, see the afterword to this book. It is surely not by chance that Tassin took his reference to *stasis* from Plato's *Republic*: the politics put forward in this work aims not only at the elimination of conflict, but also of the *diversity* of interpretations of the law. It is because, according to Plato, this diversity is the enemy of what should be the unity of the city-state, that he condemns poets and theatre along with painting, writing and the Phrygian mode in music – from which the *triton diabolicum* is fundamental for the *Blues*, the black American musical form, as well as being the source for that Jazz which Adorno found it so difficult to follow – far too unexpected for him, no doubt.

24 This is essentially what I sought to establish in the first two volumes of *Technics and Time*.

25 This grammatization is an epoch of the gramme, theorized by Jacques Derrida in *De la grammatologie* (Paris: Minuit, 1967). The concept of grammatization put forward by Sylvain Auroux – which owes a lot to Derrida's work, whatever he says – calls for the complexification of Derridian grammatology, particularly regarding the integration of the prosthesis of tertiary retentions. This is something I sketched out in 'La fidélité aux limites de la déconstruction et les prothèses de la foi' ['Fidelity to the Limits of Deconstruction and the Prostheses of Faith'], *Alter*, no. 8, ENS de Fontenay, 2000, p. 199.

26 See *Technics and Time 3: Cinematic Time and the Question of Malaise*.

27 This translates 'travail en miettes' (literally 'work in crumbs') and refers to the title of Georges Friedmann's 1956 study of the effects of technological progress on work. The fragmentation refers to the division of tasks on a production line [trans.].

28 See *Aimer, s'aimer, nous aimer*. This *one* certainly has its own force: as Blanchot says, 'one dies'. In this, one is the *extremity* of individuation, individuation at its limit, and in this a kind of *truth* of individuation. This is the force of misery. But this can only be a force as a thought *of* misery, and of the *misery of thought* – and the *profoundly stupid conditions* of thought, stupidity, that is, on the occasion of the default of the origin constitutive of the originary technicity of the *genus* that *we* perhaps still are. I will develop this point in *Symbolic Misery 2: The* Catastrophe *of the Sensible*.

29 On this illness of the *we*, cf. Barbara Stiegler, *Nietzsche et la critique de la chair* [*Nietzsche and the Critique of Flesh*] (Paris: PUF, 2005).

30 For a detailed exposition of this idea, see *Technics and Time 3: Cinematic Time and the Question of Malaise*, p. 138.

31 *Technics and Time 3: Cinematic Time and the Question of Malaise*, p. 138.

32 *Negotiations*, p.180.

33 On all these questions, see *Aimer, s'aimer, nous aimer*.

34 The first part of this sentence translates 'C'est la débandade', which on its own means 'It's complete chaos'. However, in the second part of the sentence Stiegler is playing with one of the meanings of the verb 'débander' – to lose one's erection – hence the references to Viagra and pornography [trans.].

35 See below and *Symbolic Misery 2: The* Catastrophe *of the Sensible*.

36 See *Technics and Time 3: Cinematic Time and the Question of Malaise.*
37 On the question of consumption as the modern modality of adoption, see *Technics and Time 3: Cinematic Time and the Question of Malaise*, ch. III.
38 On this point, see *Technics and Time 1: The Fault of Epimetheus.*
39 Naomi Klein, *No Logo* (London: Picador, 1999) and Jeremy Rifkin, *The Age of Access* (London: Penguin, 2001).
40 *The Age of Access*, p. 94. The French translation begins 'C'est la capacité d'*attention* de consommateurs . . .'. The translation therefore makes a direct reference to consumers here, which is rather implied in the English. The italics are Stiegler's [trans.].
41 Gilles Deleuze and Felix Guattari, *A Thousand Plateaus*, translated by Brian Massumi (London: The Athlone Press, 1988).
42 On these questions, see Gilles Deleuze, *Difference and Repetition*, translated by Paul Patton (New York: Columbia University Press, 1994). We underline here that an apparatus of capture may very well be entropic.
43 These relations between retentions and protentions are determined by the synthesis of recognition defined by Kant in the *Critique of Pure Reason*, but as I have criticized it from the perspective of the concept of tertiary retentions. What is protended in the retained will be analysed as a game of stereotypes and traumatypes in *La Technique et le Temps 5. Le défaut qu'il faut* [*Technics and Time 5: Necessary Default*] (forthcoming).
44 I developed this thesis, particularly in *Technics and Time 1: The Fault of Epimetheus.*
45 I have already spoken of this development in *Technics and Time 1.* On this point, see also Pascal Jolivet in *Vers un capitalisme cognitif* [*Towards a Cognitive Capitalism*], edited by Christian Azaïs, Antonella Corsani and Patrick Dieuaide (Paris: Harmattan, 2001).
46 The Charlus bumblebee is in Proust the wasp in Chauvin and Deleuze. 'The orchid deterritorializes by forming an image, a tracing of a wasp; but the wasp reterritorializes on that image. The wasp is nevertheless deterritorialized, becoming a piece in the orchid's reproductive apparatus. But it reterritorializes the orchid by transporting its pollen. Wasp and orchid, as heterogeneous elements, form a rhizome' (Gilles Deleuze and Felix Guattari, *A Thousand Plateaus*, p. 10).
47 J.-F. Lyotard, *Libidinal Economy*, translated by Iain Hamilton Grant (Bloomington, IN: Indiana University Press, 1993).

48   See *Technics and Time 3: Cinematic Time and the Question of Malaise*, ch. III; and 'Les guerres du temps' ['The Wars of Time'] in *La Ville en continue* [*The Continuous City*], edited by Luc Gwiazdzinski (La Tour d'Aigues: Datar/Editions de l'Aube, 2003).

49   *Negotiations*, p. 182.

50   Cited by André Gorz in *L'Immatériel* (Paris: Galilée, 2003).

51   Aristotle, *On the Soul* (Harvard, MA: Loeb Classical Library, 1957). On this point, see Bernard Stiegler, *Acting Out*, translated by David Barison and Daniel Ross (Stanford, CA: Stanford University Press, 2008).

52   Gilbert Simondon, *Du mode d'existence des objects techniques* [*On the Mode of Existence of Technical Objects*], p. 247. For a very extensive commentary, see J.-H. Barthélémy, *Sens et connaissance à partir et en-deçà de Simondon* [*Meaning and Knowledge From and Before Simondon*].

53   On this triplicity, see also Nicholas Salzmann, MA thesis, Sciences humaines et technologiques, Université de technologie de Compiègne, 1994.

54   This is what Marxism was *unable to think* as it *opposed* infrastructures to superstructures.

55   'Within the space of a few decades the social memory had engulfed in books the whole of antiquity, the history of the great peoples, the geography and ethnography of a world now definitely acknowledged to be round, philosophy, law, the sciences, the arts, the study of technics, and a literature translated from twenty different languages. The ever-widening stream still flows today, but at no moment in human history did the collective memory dilate more rapidly than in the eighteenth century in Europe' (André Leroi-Gourhan, *Gesture and Speech*, translated by Anna Bostock Berger (Cambridge, MA: Massachusetts Institute of Technology Press, 1993), p. 262).

56   Leroi-Gourhan, *Gesture and Speech*, p. 262.

57   This has doubtless been under way since the opening of modernity: I will come back to it in *Symbolic Misery 2: The Catastrophe of the Sensible*. But the integration of the system of production with the mnemotological system dates from the end of the twentieth century: this is precisely what constitutes hyper-industrialization.

58   See Bernard Stiegler, ' "Sociétés d'auteurs" et "sémantiques situées" ' ['societies of authors' and 'situated semantics'], in *Des alexandrins II. Les métamorphoses du lecteur*, ed. Ch. Jacob (Paris: Bibliothèque nationale de France, 2001) p. 297.

59   In *Ecographies: Of Television*, filmed interviews with Jacques Derrida, translated by Jennifer Bajorek (Cambridge: Polity, 2002), ch. 3.

60   As suggested by Olivier Lartillot in the seminar I run at Ircam. See above Ch. III, n. 12.

61   SGML, HTML, XML, MPEG, VRML, etc.: so many norms of grammatization of the symbolic activity making up the trans-individual reality of collective and psychic individuation.

62   See *Technics and Time 3: Cinematic Time and the Question of Malaise*, p. 211.

63   *Gesture and Speech*, p. 349.

64   See *Gesture and Speech* and *Technics and Time 1: The Fault of Epimetheus*, pp. 169–72.

65   'Les sociétés de fourmis: régulation et apprentissage' ['Ant Societies: Regulation and learning'] *Les systèmes multi-agents*, seminar organized by Charles Lenay at the université de technologie de Compiègne.

66   Dominique Lestel, 'Fourmis cybernétiques et robot-insectes: social-ité et cognition à l'interface de la robotique et l'éthologie ex-périmentale' [Cybernetic Ants and Robot-Insects: Sociality and Cognition at the Interface of Robotics and Experimental Ethology'], *Information sur les sciences sociales*, 31, 2, 1992, pp. 179–211.

67   *Technics and Time 2: Disorientation*, p. 167.

68   *Gesture and Speech*, p. 349.

69   See B. Stiegler, 'La désincarnation', in *Penser les réseaux* [*Thinking Networks*], edited by Daniel Parrochia (Seyselle: Champs Vallon, 2000).

70   Sigmund Freud, *Civilisation and its Discontents*, translated by David McLintock (London: Penguin Books, 2002) p. 60.

71   On this question of composition, see *Aimer, s'aimer, nous aimer*, pp. 36–7 and above all pp. 74–5.

72   See *Aimer, s'aimer, nous aimer*, pp. 74–5.

73   Thelonious Monk spoke of music as he understood it [*telle qu'il l'entendait*] in terms of a limp. I recall here that Oedipus limped, as did, for that matter, his Labdacide ancestors – a theme I will come back to in *Technics and Time 4* (forthcoming).

IV   Tiresias and the War of Time

1   Gilles Châtelet, *Vivre et penser comme des porcs* [*Living and Thinking like Pigs*] (Paris: Exils, 1998).

2   'Our thoughts, values, every "yes", "no", "if" and "but" grow from us with the same inevitability as fruits borne on the tree – all related and referring to one another and a testimonial to *one* will, *one* health, *one* earth, *one* sun. – Do *you* like the taste of our fruit? – But

of what concern is that to the trees? And of what concern is it to *us* philosophers? . . .' (Friedrich Nietzsche, *On the Genealogy of Morality*, preface, para. 2).

3   On this point, see *Aimer, s'aimer, nous aimer.*

4   This nightmare aesthetic was on display at the 2003 Lyon Biennale and is also to be found in *Dancer in the Dark* and *Dogville* (Lars Von Trier), *La Vie de Jesus* (Bruno Dumont), *The Matrix* and, especially, *Elephant*, as well as other products which seem to be the reality of the nightmare itself, to whatever extent they draw inspiration from philosophical models. It is also an expression of the necessity of reconstituting experience when it has been destroyed, including as experience of life, of the reality of existence where military camps, for example, are shown on the television, suddenly to be neutralized by the fact of being shown. It is in this way that I encountered the horrifying installation *Sod and Sodie Sock Comp. O.S.O* (1998) by Mike Kelly and Paul McCarthy at the Lyon Biennale. Here, at the edge of the nightmare of the blinding image, the work of Pascal Convert is also to be found.

5   Especially by way of DRMS, or Digital Rights Management Systems.

6   Jean-Michel Frodon, *La Projection nationale. Cinéma et nation* [*National Projection: Cinema and Nation*] (Paris: Odile Jacob, 1998), p. 145.

7   To the roses inasmuch as they are *artificial* flowers, which is to say just as much as *beauty itself* than as *flowers of evil* [*fleurs de mal*].

8   Jean-Luc Godard, *Introduction à une véritable histoire du cinéma* (Paris: Albatros, 1980), p. 209.

9   *Signes et perroquets*, an installation first displayed in Cannes by Alain Fleischer, staged this projection of the *I* that only takes place on the condition that it is also that of a *we*, at the Pompidou Centre in November 2003.

10 No more than there is meaning [*signifiant*] or non-meaning [*insignifiant*] in itself. See Bernard Stiegler, *Acting Out*.

11 'It is quite clear which colour is a hundred times more important for genealogists than blue: namely *grey*, which is to say, that which can be documented, which can actually be confirmed and has actually existed, in short, the whole, long, hard-to-decipher hieroglyphic script of man's moral past!' (Friedrich Nietzsche, *On the Genealogy of Morality*, preface, para. 7).

12 Vivien Leigh was imposed on Kazan by the production company, Kazan having originally shown *A Streetcar Named Desire* in the theatre, with Marlon Brando but without this actress. It is certain, however, that Kazan profited artistically from *Gone with*

the Wind: he made the best of his bad luck, a virtue from necessity, in short, a necessity from an accident, which is what art always is in essence.

13 And Oedipus punctures his own eyes.

Afterword

1 *Tout arrivé*, a France Culture show presented by Marc Voinchet and broadcast on 8 December 2003.

2 See Ch. I, n. 21 [trans.].

3 See Jacques Derrida, *Béliers. Le dialogue ininterrompu: entre deux infinis, le poème* [*Aries, The Uninterrupted Dialogue between Two Infinites, the Poem*] (Paris: Galilée, 2003).

4 See Bernard Stiegler, *Acting Out*.

5 Hannah Arendt, *The Human Condition* (Chicago, IL: University of Chicago Press, 1998).

6 Karl Marx, *Critique of Hegel's Philosophy of Right*, translated by Joseph O'Malley (Oxford: Oxford University Press, 1970), where he denounces 'logical mysticism', principally as the annulment of singularity, and where he writes that in Hegelian right, 'The universal appears everywhere as a determinate particular thing, while the individual [*singulier* in the French translation] nowhere arrives at his true universality.'

Index